HEALING YOUR WOUNDED INNER CHILD

A Guide to Reparenting Yourself and Finding Emotional Freedom

Amelia Fellows

Table of Contents

Introduction

What is Inner Child Recovery?

Inner Child Recovery is the process of reconnecting with and healing the part of yourself that still carries the emotions, beliefs, and wounds from your childhood. Your inner child represents your younger self—the one who experienced joy, curiosity, wonder, but also pain, fear, and unmet needs. Often, these experiences from the past can unconsciously influence your thoughts, behaviors, and emotional responses as an adult.

Through inner child recovery, you create a bridge between your adult self and this younger part of you, allowing healing, understanding, and nurturing to take place. By addressing your inner child, you can uncover the roots of self-doubt, anxiety, perfectionism, or feelings of unworthiness. You gain the opportunity to break free from patterns that no longer serve you and replace them with compassion, strength, and empowerment.

This journey is not about blaming others or reliving trauma—it's about creating a safe space within yourself to acknowledge, heal, and transform. It's a courageous act of self-love and self-discovery, where you embrace the full spectrum of who you are.

The Importance of Reconnecting with Your Inner Child

Many of us unknowingly suppress or neglect our inner child. Over time, this disconnect can manifest as emotional struggles, strained relationships, or feeling "stuck" in life. Reconnecting with your inner child is a profound way to address these underlying issues.

Why is it so important?

1. **Healing Old Wounds**: By acknowledging your inner child's pain and unmet needs, you can release the emotional baggage that may be holding you back.
2. **Building Self-Acceptance**: Reconnection allows you to embrace your vulnerabilities and imperfections, fostering greater self-love.
3. **Regaining Joy and Creativity**: Your inner child is the source of spontaneity, imagination, and joy. By reconnecting, you open yourself up to a fuller, more vibrant life.
4. **Breaking Cycles**: Many harmful patterns and coping mechanisms stem from unresolved childhood issues. Healing your inner child helps you break these cycles and build healthier habits.

Through this process, you can create a sense of inner wholeness and develop emotional resilience that serves you throughout your life.

Reconnecting with your inner child is not just a healing practice—it's a transformative journey that allows you to rediscover your authentic self.

Setting Intentions for Your Healing Journey

Before you begin this workbook, it's important to set intentions for what you hope to gain from this process. Intentions act as a guiding light, helping you stay focused and motivated as you explore the various exercises and reflections in this journey.

Start by asking yourself:

- What do I want to heal or understand about myself?
- How can I offer myself more love and care during this process?
- What do I need to let go of to grow into the person I want to be?

When setting your intentions:

1. **Be Honest**: Allow yourself to dream big but also acknowledge your fears or doubts. Healing is not linear, and it's okay to take small steps.
2. **Be Compassionate**: Treat yourself as you would a close friend. This is a time for nurturing, not criticism.
3. **Be Open**: This workbook may uncover emotions or memories you didn't expect. Be willing to approach them with curiosity and patience.

As you embark on this journey, remember to celebrate every step forward—no matter how small. The act of showing up for yourself is already a huge accomplishment.

Part 1:

Understanding the Inner Child

1: Who Is Your Inner Child?

Your inner child is the part of you that carries the emotional and psychological imprints from your childhood experiences. It's the essence of who you were as a child—the playful, curious, sensitive, and authentic part of you that once experienced the world with wonder and vulnerability. This part of you holds both the joy and the wounds from your earliest years, and it influences how you perceive the world, handle emotions, and relate to others as an adult.

As you grow, many people tend to suppress or disconnect from their inner child as a way of coping with the challenges of life. Whether it's due to difficult childhood experiences, trauma, or the demands of adulthood, the inner child often retreats into the subconscious, but it doesn't disappear. Instead, it continues to affect you in subtle or overt ways.

The inner child is not just a reflection of past experiences but a living, active part of you. It's the core of your emotional world, and when it's healed, it opens the door to greater self-compassion, emotional freedom, and authenticity. Understanding and reconnecting with your inner child can be a powerful path to healing and self-discovery.

Characteristics of Your Inner Child:

1. **Vulnerable**: The inner child holds the emotions and pain of childhood, including fear, sadness, shame, and abandonment. It is a sensitive part of you that craves love and safety.
2. **Creative and Playful**: As children, we are naturally imaginative, curious, and playful. Your inner child holds these qualities, helping you connect to your creativity, joy, and spontaneity.
3. **Authentic and Truthful**: Children are naturally authentic; they don't yet learn to mask or hide their emotions. Your inner child can help you rediscover your true self and embrace your feelings without judgment.
4. **Fearful and Protective**: Your inner child may carry fears based on past experiences, such as fear of rejection, failure, or abandonment. It may also hold protective mechanisms that helped you survive difficult situations.
5. **Eager for Love**: Your inner child yearns for acceptance, love, and attention. Whether or not it received these things in childhood, it still seeks them now. Healing your inner child involves offering it the love and care it may not have received.

How Does Your Inner Child Show Up in Your Adult Life?

Your inner child may show up in your adult life in various ways—sometimes without you even realizing it. You might notice certain emotional patterns or triggers that stem from childhood experiences. These can manifest as:

- **Emotional Reactivity**: You may have strong emotional reactions to situations that seem disproportionate to the present moment. This could be a sign that your inner child's wounds are being triggered.
- **People-Pleasing or Perfectionism**: If you were conditioned as a child to seek approval or avoid criticism, your inner child may still push you to be overly pleasing or perfect, even as an adult.
- **Difficulty Setting Boundaries**: If your inner child grew up in an environment where boundaries were not respected or were unclear, you may struggle with asserting yourself in relationships or maintaining healthy limits.
- **A Fear of Abandonment or Rejection**: If your inner child experienced neglect or emotional abandonment, you may have deep-seated fears of being left behind or not being loved.

Healing your inner child involves recognizing when these childhood patterns are showing up in your adult life and gently guiding yourself towards healthier, more compassionate responses.

2: Signs Your Inner Child Needs Healing

Your inner child is a part of you that carries both the joy and the pain of your past. When this part of you has been neglected or wounded, it can impact your emotional and mental well-being in adulthood. Recognizing the signs that your inner child needs healing is the first step toward reclaiming emotional wholeness and well-being.

Healing your inner child isn't about changing who you are but about reclaiming the lost parts of yourself and nurturing them with love, care, and understanding. When your inner child carries unresolved pain or unmet needs, it can manifest in various ways throughout your adult life. Here are some key signs that your inner child might need healing:

1. Unresolved Emotional Wounds: Many of us carry emotional wounds from childhood that have never been addressed. These wounds might stem from neglect, emotional or physical abuse, abandonment, or other forms of trauma. If you find yourself feeling overwhelmed by certain emotions, such as fear, anger, sadness, or shame, without fully understanding why, these could be signs that your inner child's wounds are still unhealed.

- **Example**: You may suddenly feel extreme anxiety in situations that seem harmless, like social events or at work, because the emotional triggers from childhood have been activated.

2. Self-Sabotaging Behaviors: If you struggle with self-destructive patterns, such as procrastination, self-criticism, or avoiding responsibilities, these behaviors may be rooted in the inner child's desire to avoid discomfort or fear of failure. Your inner child may have learned unhealthy coping mechanisms to survive in an environment where it felt unsafe or unloved.

- **Example**: You might feel the urge to give up on your dreams or avoid challenges, as your inner child may have learned early on to avoid situations where it felt inadequate or rejected.

3. Difficulty with Self-Love and Compassion: Your inner child thrives on love and acceptance. If you struggle with feelings of low self-worth or a lack of compassion for yourself, your inner child may not have received the nurturing it needed during childhood. Healing involves learning how to offer that love to yourself now, even when it's difficult.

- **Example**: You might be overly critical of yourself when you make mistakes, constantly seeking validation or approval from others, or feeling unworthy of love and care.

4. Emotional Overreactions or Intense Triggers: Sometimes, a small incident can trigger an exaggerated emotional response. This overreaction often happens because the event resonates with an old wound from your childhood. The inner child carries unprocessed emotions that get activated in the present, leading to intense feelings that seem disproportionate.

- **Example**: An argument with a friend might cause you to feel abandoned or rejected, triggering feelings from childhood where you didn't feel heard or seen.

5. Difficulty Trusting Others: Your inner child may have learned not to trust the people around it, especially if it was betrayed or let down during childhood. As an adult, you might struggle to trust others, find it hard to form deep emotional connections, or feel as though you're always on guard.

- **Example**: You might push people away, avoid intimacy, or fear being vulnerable in relationships, which stems from not having your emotional needs met as a child.

6. Repeating Unhealthy Relationship Patterns: If you find yourself stuck in toxic or unfulfilling relationships, it could be a sign that your inner child is seeking to heal through repetition. You may subconsciously recreate relationships that mimic past wounds in an attempt to resolve old issues.

- **Example**: If you grew up in an environment where love was conditional or inconsistent, you might unconsciously attract partners who reinforce this pattern of emotional instability.

7. A Fear of Being Alone or Abandoned: The inner child fears abandonment, and if this fear is not addressed, it can create a deep-seated anxiety in adulthood. You might feel terrified of being alone, having trouble spending time by yourself, or constantly seeking reassurance from others.

- **Example**: You may struggle with being alone, feeling a constant need for external validation, or being afraid that relationships will end even when things are going well.

8. Lack of Playfulness or Joy: Children naturally experience joy and playfulness, but as adults, we may lose touch with this aspect of ourselves. If you find it hard to feel joy or have fun, or if you feel overly serious and burdened by life, it could be because your inner child is still longing for the freedom and creativity it once had.

- **Example**: You may feel like you've "forgotten how to play" and struggle to do things for fun, or feel disconnected from activities that once brought you joy.

Healing Your Inner Child

Recognizing these signs is not about judgment or criticism; it's about understanding that your inner child is asking for your attention and care. The process of healing involves listening to that inner voice, acknowledging its pain, and offering the love, compassion, and nurturing it didn't receive before.

Healing your inner child is about taking small but profound steps to integrate this part of yourself, creating a relationship of trust, care, and unconditional love.

3: The Roots of Inner Child Wounds

Inner child wounds are deeply rooted in the experiences, emotional neglect, or trauma that you endured during your early years. These wounds are often formed when your emotional needs as a child were not fully met or when you were subjected to negative or harmful experiences. The experiences that shape your inner child wounds are unique to each person, but there are common roots from which these wounds often stem. Understanding the origins of your inner child's wounds is the first step toward healing, as it allows you to gain insight into how these early experiences have shaped your adult behaviors, emotional reactions, and beliefs.

1. Childhood Trauma and Abuse: Trauma experienced during childhood—whether physical, emotional, or sexual abuse—leaves deep scars that affect your emotional and psychological well-being throughout life. Children who endure trauma often struggle with feelings of shame, guilt, fear, or confusion. These experiences create a fracture in the child's sense of safety and trust in the world.

- **Physical Abuse**: If you were physically hurt or witnessed violence, your inner child may carry wounds of fear, helplessness, and distrust in the safety of others.
- **Emotional Abuse**: Verbal attacks, neglect, or manipulation can lead your inner child to feel unloved, unworthy, or invisible.

Emotional abuse often teaches children to suppress their feelings and to hide their true selves.

- **Sexual Abuse**: This creates profound feelings of shame, guilt, confusion, and often a loss of innocence. The inner child who experiences sexual trauma may develop a distorted view of their own body and emotional boundaries.

Impact in Adulthood: The trauma from childhood can lead to issues such as anxiety, depression, a constant feeling of being unsafe, difficulty trusting others, and difficulty setting healthy emotional boundaries.

2. **Emotional Neglect:** Emotional neglect occurs when a child's emotional needs—such as affection, attention, validation, and comfort—are not met, even if the child's basic physical needs (food, shelter) are provided. Children who grow up in emotionally neglectful environments may feel invisible, unloved, and unimportant. This can lead to an inner child that feels abandoned, unworthy of love, or incapable of receiving affection.

- **Lack of Affection**: Children who don't receive physical affection, such as hugs or praise, may struggle with feelings of loneliness and emotional deprivation.
- **Emotional Unavailability**: When caregivers are emotionally distant or unavailable, children may feel emotionally neglected and develop a belief that their feelings don't matter.

- **Inconsistent Nurturance**: If affection and care are given inconsistently, the child may feel unsure of their worth and develop insecurity.

Impact in Adulthood: You might experience difficulty expressing your emotions, feeling unworthy of love, or developing unhealthy attachment patterns in relationships. You may also struggle with self-soothing, as your inner child may not have learned how to meet its own emotional needs.

3. Abandonment and Loss: Abandonment can take many forms, from physical abandonment (e.g., one or both parents leaving) to emotional abandonment (e.g., emotionally distant or unavailable caregivers). If a child experiences the loss of a parent, a significant caregiver, or even a close friend, it can create a deep sense of insecurity, fear, and unhealed grief.

- **Parental Separation or Divorce**: If your parents separated or divorced when you were young, you may have felt rejected or abandoned, even if you weren't directly abandoned by either parent. The emotional fallout of separation can have lasting effects.
- **Death of a Caregiver**: The death of a parent or caregiver can lead to deep grief and feelings of abandonment, even if the child is surrounded by other caregivers.

- **Emotional Unavailability**: Even if a parent or caregiver is physically present, if they are emotionally unavailable, it can create a sense of abandonment in the child.

Impact in Adulthood: You might struggle with a fear of abandonment in relationships, difficulty trusting others, and anxiety about losing people you love. You may also experience attachment issues, such as clinginess or avoidance in romantic relationships.

4. Unmet Needs for Validation and Encouragement: Children thrive when they are validated and encouraged. This validation helps them develop healthy self-esteem, self-worth, and confidence. When children grow up without receiving adequate validation for their efforts or emotions, they may internalize a belief that they are not good enough.

- **Lack of Praise or Encouragement**: If your accomplishments, big or small, went unnoticed or were downplayed, you may have developed feelings of inadequacy and a need for external validation.
- **Perfectionism**: A child who never receives approval for their efforts may learn that they must be perfect in order to be loved or accepted. This can lead to perfectionistic tendencies later in life.
- **Lack of Emotional Support**: Without proper emotional support, children may struggle to process their feelings in

healthy ways, leading to emotional suppression or outbursts as adults.

Impact in Adulthood: As an adult, you may have trouble accepting compliments, feel insecure about your abilities, or strive for perfection. You might also seek validation externally rather than internally, never feeling fully satisfied with your own achievements.

5. Conditional Love and Approval

In some cases, love and approval from caregivers or authority figures may be conditional on the child's behavior or performance. This creates the belief that love must be earned, and it can lead to deep-seated feelings of unworthiness and anxiety.

- **Conditional Love**: If you were only loved or accepted when you behaved a certain way or achieved certain things, you might have grown up with the belief that you're only lovable when you're "good enough."
- **Overly Critical Caregivers**: When caregivers or authority figures are overly critical or demanding, a child may internalize a belief that they are not enough as they are.
- **Favoritism or Comparison**: If you were compared to siblings or others, or if one child was favored over another, it can cause feelings of resentment, jealousy, and a belief that you are not worthy of love.

Impact in Adulthood: You might struggle with a fear of failure, perfectionism, or feelings of inadequacy. You may also experience difficulty with self-acceptance and may constantly seek external validation to feel worthy.

6. Negative Messages and Limiting Beliefs: The messages children receive from their caregivers, teachers, and others during their formative years can have a profound impact on their self-esteem and worldview. If you were constantly told you weren't good enough, that you would never succeed, or that your feelings were invalid, these negative messages can become internalized as limiting beliefs that hinder your growth and self-worth.

- **Criticism and Judgment**: Constant criticism from caregivers, teachers, or peers can lead to feelings of worthlessness or self-doubt. Children who are frequently criticized may believe that they are inherently flawed.
- **Unrealistic Expectations**: If you were held to standards that were too high or unattainable, you may have developed perfectionistic tendencies or a deep fear of failure.

Impact in Adulthood: As an adult, these limiting beliefs can cause you to self-sabotage, avoid opportunities, or constantly doubt yourself. You may feel that no matter what you do, it will never be enough.

4: Exploring Your Past

Our childhood experiences shape the lens through which we view the world, ourselves, and others. The memories we hold—both positive and negative—serve as the foundation for our emotional patterns and behaviors in adulthood. When you begin to explore your past, you may uncover memories that have been tucked away for years, often because they are too painful, confusing, or complex to process at the time.

However, revisiting these childhood memories in a safe and intentional way can help you understand the origins of your emotional wounds, patterns, and beliefs. By exploring your past, you can reconnect with the inner child who still carries these memories, offering it the compassion, healing, and support it may not have received in the past

The Power of Childhood Memories

Childhood memories are not just snapshots of past events but are deeply connected to your emotional and psychological development. These memories form the core of your beliefs about yourself, your self-worth, and your relationships with others. They also affect your responses to stress, your emotional triggers, and the way you navigate the world.

Some memories may feel like "happy moments"—times when you felt safe, loved, and connected. These memories can serve as a source of strength and self-assurance as you heal. On the other hand, painful memories—such as those involving trauma, neglect, or loss—can leave scars that influence your behavior and emotions long into adulthood. By acknowledging and processing these memories, you begin to heal the inner child that was affected by them.

Types of Childhood Memories to Explore

When exploring your past, it's helpful to consider different types of memories that may have impacted your emotional development. Not all memories are negative; some are neutral or positive, and they also play a significant role in your inner child's healing.

- **Positive Memories**: These are memories where you felt loved, safe, supported, and valued. Reconnecting with these memories helps you rediscover your sense of worth and inner joy.
    - **Example**: A memory of a family vacation, receiving praise for a small achievement, or moments of unconditional love from a caregiver.
- **Negative Memories**: These memories often hold the emotional wounds from your past—moments when you felt abandoned, criticized, hurt, or neglected. These memories are often tied to deep feelings of fear, shame, or anger.
    - **Example**: A memory of being ignored by a caregiver, facing emotional or physical punishment, or feeling rejected by a parent.

- **Neutral Memories**: These memories might not stand out emotionally but are still important because they reflect the everyday life you lived as a child. Sometimes, neutral memories reveal patterns of behavior or coping mechanisms that you developed to survive in a difficult environment.
    - **Example**: Routine events like going to school, interactions with classmates, or family dynamics that were not necessarily abusive but felt emotionally distant.

The Emotional Impact of Childhood Memories

When you begin to examine childhood memories, you may experience strong emotional reactions. These reactions can range from sadness and anger to joy and relief. The emotional impact of these memories is significant because it helps you understand how your inner child processed those events and how it may still be carrying those emotions today.

- **Repressed Memories**: Some memories may have been repressed as a form of self-protection. This is common in cases of trauma or emotional neglect. When repressed memories surface, they may be accompanied by feelings of confusion, anger, or sadness.
- **Unhealed Emotional Pain**: Memories tied to past wounds may evoke feelings of abandonment, shame, guilt, or fear.

These emotions may continue to affect your adult life, even if you consciously don't recall the events.

- **Joyful Memories**: Positive memories can evoke feelings of warmth, love, and connection. These memories serve as reminders of the happiness and joy that you once felt and can be a source of healing and comfort in the present.

Identifying Patterns in Your Childhood Memories

As you explore your childhood memories, you may begin to identify patterns that reflect certain beliefs or behaviors you developed as a result of those experiences. These patterns may still show up in your adult life, influencing how you relate to others, handle challenges, or perceive your own worth.

- **People-Pleasing**: If your childhood memories include times when you felt the need to please others to gain love or approval, you may have developed people-pleasing behaviors as an adult.
- **Perfectionism**: Memories of high expectations or conditional love might have led to a deep-rooted belief that you must be perfect in order to be loved and accepted.
- **Trust Issues**: If you were emotionally or physically abandoned, or if trust was broken in childhood, you might struggle with trust in your adult relationships.

- **Fear of Rejection**: Experiences of emotional or physical rejection as a child can lead to a lifelong fear of being abandoned, ignored, or left out.

By understanding these patterns, you can begin to break free from old habits and create new, healthier ways of coping and relating to others.

Healing Through Revisiting Childhood Memories

Healing your inner child involves revisiting your childhood memories with compassion, patience, and a willingness to understand the emotional impact they had on you. Rather than ignoring or suppressing painful memories, healing requires acknowledging their existence and providing the love, care, and attention your younger self may have lacked.

- **Self-Compassion**: When you remember the pain of your childhood, treat yourself with kindness and understanding. Recognize that you did the best you could with the resources and coping mechanisms available to you at the time.
- **Reframing Memories**: Try to look at your childhood experiences through a compassionate lens, acknowledging that the actions of others were often influenced by their own wounds and limitations. You can start to reframe your memories, seeing yourself as a child who deserved love and care, even if that wasn't always provided.

- **Inner Dialogue**: Engage in a compassionate dialogue with your inner child. Talk to your younger self as if you were there for them at that time, offering the comfort, support, and protection they may have needed.

Part 2:

Uncovering Your Inner Child's Voice

5: Recalling Forgotten Emotions

Our childhood is a time when emotions can be overwhelming and difficult to process, especially when those emotions are ignored, invalidated, or repressed. As a result, many feelings from the past are buried deep within the subconscious, hidden from conscious awareness. These forgotten emotions are often connected to unresolved pain, trauma, or unmet needs, and they continue to affect our adult lives in ways we may not fully understand.

Reconnecting with and recalling these forgotten emotions is an essential part of healing the inner child. By bringing these feelings to light, you allow yourself to fully experience, understand, and release them, paving the way for emotional growth, self-compassion, and personal transformation.

Why Do We Forget Emotions?

Emotions are powerful, and when we experience overwhelming or painful emotions, our mind may try to protect us by suppressing or repressing them. As children, we don't have the emotional tools or coping mechanisms to process complex feelings like fear, anger, shame, or sadness. Instead, we may push them down or ignore them to survive difficult situations.

- **Repression as Protection**: The mind may repress emotions that are too painful or intense for a child to process at the time. This can happen in cases of trauma or neglect, where the emotional experience is simply too much to handle.
- **Emotional Unavailability**: If caregivers were emotionally unavailable or unable to help you process your feelings, you may have learned to suppress your emotions in order to avoid conflict, criticism, or rejection.
- **Survival Mechanism**: Sometimes, emotional repression is a survival strategy. If your environment was unsafe or unpredictable, ignoring or disconnecting from emotions could have been a way to cope and navigate daily life without getting overwhelmed.

Over time, these forgotten emotions remain stored in the body and mind, influencing your emotional reactions, relationships, and behavior as an adult. The task now is to bring these emotions back into conscious awareness so that you can fully heal and release them.

Recognizing Forgotten Emotions

You may not consciously remember every emotional experience from childhood, but certain situations, memories, or feelings in adulthood may trigger forgotten emotions. The key is to pay attention to emotional patterns that arise in your present life.

- **Unexplained Emotional Reactions**: If you react strongly to seemingly minor events, such as feeling disproportionately angry or anxious about something small, this may be a clue that a forgotten emotion from your past is being triggered.
- **Physical Symptoms**: Your body often holds onto emotions that the mind has forgotten. Tension in your shoulders, stomachaches, headaches, or chronic pain can be physical manifestations of unresolved emotions.
- **Overwhelming Feelings in Relationships**: If you struggle with relationships, such as feeling overly dependent on others or having intense fears of abandonment, it may indicate that unprocessed emotions from childhood are influencing your present-day interactions.
- **Frequent Mood Swings**: If you find yourself fluctuating between emotional extremes—feeling very high one moment and very low the next—there may be suppressed emotions bubbling to the surface, demanding attention and healing.

These emotional triggers are signals from your inner child, asking you to pay attention and explore what lies beneath the surface.

How Forgotten Emotions Affect Our Adult Lives

The forgotten emotions from childhood often show up in adulthood as unresolved wounds that influence your actions, relationships, and mental health. Even if you've forgotten the initial cause of these feelings, they can still have a profound impact on your life.

- **Emotional Baggage**: Unprocessed emotions can accumulate over time, creating emotional baggage that you carry into adult relationships and situations. These unresolved feelings can create patterns of emotional overreaction, miscommunication, or withdrawal.
- **Self-Sabotage**: Forgotten emotions can lead to self-sabotaging behaviors, such as pushing people away, avoiding success, or settling for less than you deserve. These behaviors are often rooted in feelings of unworthiness, fear, or shame that you may not even consciously recognize.
- **Anxiety and Depression**: The weight of forgotten emotions can manifest as anxiety, depression, or chronic stress. These emotions often stem from unresolved pain that has been buried for too long, and they need to be processed in order to heal.

Techniques for Recalling Forgotten Emotions

Recalling forgotten emotions involves safely revisiting your past and creating space for those emotions to surface. It's important to approach this process with patience, self-compassion, and a willingness to feel vulnerable.

- **Journaling**: Writing can be a powerful tool for accessing and processing forgotten emotions. Journaling allows you to express feelings that may be difficult to verbalize. Try writing freely about memories or situations that come to mind, paying attention to any feelings or sensations that arise.
    - **Prompts**: "What memories come up when I think about my childhood? What emotions do I feel when I remember specific people or events? How did I cope with difficult emotions at the time?"
- **Visualization**: In a quiet and calm space, close your eyes and visualize yourself as a child. Revisit moments from your childhood, allowing yourself to feel whatever emotions arise. Don't judge or try to control the emotions—simply observe and acknowledge them.
- **Mindfulness and Body Scanning**: Mindfulness practices can help you become aware of emotions stored in your body. By scanning your body from head to toe, you can identify areas of tension, discomfort, or pain, which may indicate unresolved emotions. Pay attention to what emotions surface as you focus on each area of your body.
- **Therapy and Guided Healing**: Working with a therapist or counselor trained in inner child healing can be incredibly helpful in recalling forgotten emotions. Guided therapy techniques, such as inner child work, can provide a safe space for you to connect with your emotions and explore your past.

Processing Forgotten Emotions

Once forgotten emotions have been recalled, it's crucial to give yourself the space and time needed to process them. This involves feeling and expressing these emotions in a healthy, non-judgmental way.

- **Allow Yourself to Feel**: It's important to let yourself experience the emotions that surface without judgment. Remember, it's okay to feel sadness, anger, or fear. These feelings are valid and part of your healing journey.
- **Acknowledge the Child Within**: As you process forgotten emotions, imagine yourself as a child again—vulnerable and in need of comfort. Offer yourself the love and care that your inner child may not have received at the time.
- **Release and Let Go**: After processing the emotions, allow them to flow through you and release them. This may happen through tears, physical movement, or simply by letting go of the emotional charge attached to the memory.

6: Journaling to Connect with Your Inner Child

Journaling is a powerful tool for connecting with your inner child and fostering emotional healing. It creates a safe space for you to express thoughts and feelings that might otherwise be difficult to process. Writing helps you access deeper parts of your subconscious, where your inner child's emotions, needs, and experiences are stored. By journaling, you can facilitate a conversation with your younger self, offering compassion, understanding, and healing.

This practice allows you to gain insight into how your childhood experiences have shaped who you are today and begin the process of re-parenting yourself—showing love, care, and acceptance to the parts of you that need it the most.

The Healing Power of Writing

Journaling provides an opportunity to express what's hidden deep inside—emotions, fears, joys, and desires that you may not fully understand or have been able to articulate before. For your inner child, writing can feel like a direct conversation with yourself, where you can validate feelings that were previously overlooked or dismissed.

- **Safe Space for Expression**: Writing is a private and judgment-free zone. It allows you to express emotions without fear of criticism or misunderstanding. This helps build trust with your inner child, who may have been silenced or neglected in the past.

- **Clarifying Emotions**: Through journaling, you can gain clarity about your emotions. Writing about your experiences can reveal hidden emotions, thoughts, and beliefs that you may not have fully processed or acknowledged before.
- **Creating a Dialogue**: Journaling creates an interactive space for you to "talk" to your inner child. You can ask questions, provide support, and explore the memories that have influenced your emotional development.

How to Start Journaling with Your Inner Child

To connect with your inner child through journaling, it's important to create an environment that fosters emotional safety and openness. Here are some ways to begin:

- **Set the Scene**: Find a quiet, comfortable space where you can write without distractions. Light a candle, play soothing music, or engage in other rituals that help you feel relaxed and present.
- **Speak to Your Inner Child**: When you begin journaling, address your writing directly to your inner child. You can use their name or simply refer to them as "you" to establish an intimate connection. For example: "Dear Little Me, I know you're feeling scared right now..."

- **Be Compassionate**: Approach your inner child with kindness and empathy. Let go of judgment and perfectionism—your inner child needs love and acceptance, not criticism. If you're revisiting painful memories, acknowledge that your younger self did the best they could under difficult circumstances.
- **Write Freely**: Don't worry about grammar, structure, or spelling—just let the words flow. Write from the heart, allowing yourself to express whatever comes up. Trust that whatever arises is important.

Prompts to Get You Started

Sometimes it can be hard to know where to begin. To guide your journaling practice, here are a few prompts to help you connect with your inner child:

- **Memory Exploration**: "Can you remember a time when you felt really safe and loved as a child? What happened, and how did you feel in that moment?"
- **Feelings and Needs**: "What are you feeling right now? What does your inner child need from you in this moment?"
- **Unmet Needs**: "Was there a time in your childhood when you needed something—love, comfort, validation—that wasn't given to you? How can you provide that for your inner child now?"

- **Healing Conversations**: "If you could talk to your younger self, what would you say to offer comfort and reassurance? What would your younger self want to hear from you?"
- **Messages of Love**: "Write a letter from your adult self to your inner child, offering love, encouragement, and compassion. Let your inner child know they are safe now."

Benefits of Journaling with Your Inner Child

Journaling provides several profound benefits in the healing process:

- **Emotional Release**: Writing helps release bottled-up emotions, whether they're anger, sadness, or fear. Journaling creates a space for these emotions to flow, allowing you to process and let them go.
- **Healing the Past**: By revisiting painful memories with a compassionate perspective, journaling helps you reframe your past experiences and heal emotional wounds. This process encourages forgiveness—both for yourself and others—and helps release the emotional charge of past events.
- **Building Self-Awareness**: Journaling fosters greater self-awareness, allowing you to identify recurring patterns, triggers, and beliefs that stem from childhood wounds. By recognizing these patterns, you can begin to break free from them and create healthier ways of living and relating.

- **Reconnecting with Joy**: Writing about moments of happiness and love from your childhood can rekindle positive emotions and reawaken feelings of joy, playfulness, and freedom. This helps nourish your inner child and bring more lightness into your life.

Overcoming Resistance to Journaling

It's common to feel resistance when starting a journaling practice, especially if you're confronted with painful memories or emotions. Here are a few tips for overcoming that resistance:

- **Be Gentle with Yourself**: If you feel overwhelmed or emotionally triggered, it's okay to take a break. You can always return to your journal later when you feel ready. There's no rush in the healing process.
- **Small Steps**: If journaling feels too daunting, start with just a few minutes each day. You don't need to write for hours—small, consistent efforts can lead to big breakthroughs over time.
- **Accept All Emotions**: If painful emotions come up while journaling, let them flow. It's normal to feel discomfort, but the key is to allow yourself to experience those feelings without pushing them away. The more you allow, the more healing can take place.

7: Recognizing Limiting Beliefs Stemming from Childhood

Limiting beliefs are deeply ingrained thought patterns or convictions that hold you back from reaching your full potential. They often form in childhood, influenced by the experiences, messages, and beliefs we encounter from our parents, caregivers, teachers, and society. These beliefs become internalized and shape the way we view ourselves, others, and the world around us.

In many cases, limiting beliefs arise from negative experiences, unmet needs, or emotional wounds from childhood. They can often go unnoticed, running in the background of your mind and influencing your thoughts, behaviors, and decisions. Recognizing these limiting beliefs is the first step toward transforming them and healing the inner child.

How Limiting Beliefs Develop in Childhood

During childhood, our brains are highly impressionable and absorb information from every environment we are exposed to. The people around us, especially authority figures like parents, teachers, and caregivers, shape how we view ourselves and the world. If you grew up in an environment where love, attention, and validation were conditional, or where fear and criticism were common, your developing mind may have internalized beliefs that limit your growth and happiness.

- **Parental Messages**: Parents or caregivers, whether intentionally or unintentionally, may have passed on limiting beliefs. For example, a parent who constantly told you that you weren't good enough or could never succeed might have planted seeds of self-doubt and fear.
- **Cultural and Societal Influence**: Children also absorb beliefs and expectations from the culture and society they grow up in. This could involve messages about gender roles, appearance, achievement, and social status.
- **Traumatic Experiences**: Negative experiences, such as bullying, neglect, or abandonment, can lead to the formation of limiting beliefs about your worth, safety, or ability to trust others.

These beliefs become "truths" in your mind, and as you grow older, they continue to shape your decisions, actions, and relationships—even if you're not consciously aware of them.

Common Limiting Beliefs Formed in Childhood

Limiting beliefs often stem from childhood wounds and can manifest in various ways. Here are some common limiting beliefs that may arise:

- **"I'm not good enough."**: This belief often stems from critical parenting, where a child's achievements or efforts were never enough to gain approval or love.
- **"I'm not worthy of love."**: Children who experienced neglect or emotional abandonment might internalize the belief that they are unworthy of love or care.
- **"I'm not safe."**: Growing up in an unstable or unsafe environment may lead to the belief that the world is dangerous, and you can't trust people or situations.
- **"I have to be perfect to be accepted."**: This belief may form when a child's value is only recognized through achievements or perfection, leaving them feeling like their worth is tied to performance.
- **"I have to take care of others before myself."**: This often stems from growing up in a home where the child felt responsible for others' emotions, needs, or wellbeing, potentially leading to people-pleasing tendencies in adulthood.
- **"I will always be alone."**: This belief can develop in children who experienced abandonment, rejection, or isolation, making them feel as though they can't rely on others for support.

These beliefs, though formed in childhood, continue to impact you in adulthood. They can affect your self-esteem, decision-making, relationships, and overall sense of worth.

Identifying Limiting Beliefs in Your Life

Recognizing the limiting beliefs that originated in your childhood requires introspection and awareness. Here are some steps to help you identify these beliefs:

- **Observe Patterns in Your Thoughts and Behaviors**: Pay attention to recurring negative thought patterns or behaviors in your life. Do you often feel like you're not good enough? Do you constantly seek approval or validation from others? Do you struggle with perfectionism or fear of failure? These are signs of limiting beliefs.
- **Trace the Roots of These Beliefs**: Once you notice a limiting belief, trace its origins. Ask yourself: *When did I first start thinking this way?* Reflect on your childhood and identify moments or experiences that may have contributed to this belief.
- **Examine Your Inner Dialogue**: Listen to how you speak to yourself. Do you often criticize yourself or put yourself down? The tone and content of your inner dialogue can reveal limiting beliefs that have been internalized over the years.
- **Look at Your Actions and Decisions**: Notice the choices you make in your life. Do you avoid taking risks because you feel you're not capable? Do you over-extend yourself to please

others because you fear rejection? Your actions can provide insight into the limiting beliefs that govern your behavior.

How Limiting Beliefs Affect Your Life

Limiting beliefs not only affect how you perceive yourself, but they also impact how you relate to others and navigate the world. Here are some of the ways these beliefs can show up in your life:

- **Self-Sabotage**: Limiting beliefs often lead to self-sabotaging behaviors, such as procrastination, avoidance, or giving up on goals prematurely. You might not feel worthy of success or may fear that you'll never be able to achieve your dreams.
- **Low Self-Esteem**: Beliefs like "I'm not good enough" can result in chronic feelings of inadequacy and low self-worth. This can prevent you from taking risks, setting boundaries, or pursuing your desires.
- **Difficulty in Relationships**: Limiting beliefs about love and trust, such as "I'm not worthy of love" or "People will always let me down," can make it difficult to form healthy, trusting relationships. These beliefs can also lead to insecurity and anxiety within your relationships.
- **Fear of Failure**: If you grew up in an environment where failure was met with criticism or punishment, you might develop a deep fear of making mistakes. This fear can lead to

perfectionism, avoidance, or a lack of confidence in your abilities.

Understanding how these beliefs affect your life is an important step toward breaking free from them.

Shifting Limiting Beliefs

Healing the inner child involves identifying and transforming limiting beliefs that no longer serve you. Here are a few techniques for shifting these beliefs:

- **Awareness and Acknowledgment**: The first step is recognizing the belief and acknowledging its origins. By understanding that these beliefs were formed in childhood and were a way of coping, you can begin to separate them from your true self.
- **Rewriting Your Narrative**: Once you've identified a limiting belief, challenge it by rewriting your inner narrative. For example, if you believe you're not good enough, replace that belief with affirmations such as "I am worthy of love and success."
- **Healing the Inner Child**: Talk to your inner child and reassure them that they are safe, loved, and capable. Re-parenting your inner child with positive, supportive

messages can help shift the beliefs that were once formed from pain or fear.

- **Affirmations and Self-Love**: Practice positive affirmations daily to counter the negative messages from childhood. Affirmations like "I am enough" or "I am deserving of happiness" can help rewire your thought patterns over time.
- **Therapy or Coaching**: Working with a therapist or coach trained in inner child healing can help you identify and release deeply rooted limiting beliefs. Techniques such as cognitive behavioral therapy (CBT) or EMDR (Eye Movement Desensitization and Reprocessing) can be especially helpful for transforming these beliefs.

8: Identifying Emotional Triggers

Emotional triggers are specific situations, words, behaviors, or events that cause an intense emotional reaction, often linked to past experiences or unresolved wounds. These triggers can bring up strong feelings of anger, fear, sadness, or anxiety, and often lead to responses that feel disproportionate to the situation at hand. Understanding and identifying your emotional triggers is a key step in healing your inner child, as they are often tied to unresolved childhood wounds or unmet emotional needs.

What Are Emotional Triggers?

Emotional triggers are stimuli that activate emotional responses, typically linked to past trauma or painful memories. They can manifest in various ways and might cause you to react impulsively or out of proportion to the situation. For instance, a particular tone of voice, a specific action, or even certain words can bring up feelings of anger, fear, or sadness, even though the current situation may not warrant such a reaction.

These emotional responses often feel uncontrollable or overwhelming, and they may have deep roots in your childhood experiences. Triggers can act as a reminder of past wounds, especially those connected to your inner child, and can cause you to relive old emotional patterns.

Common Sources of Emotional Triggers

Emotional triggers are highly individual, but some common sources include:

- **Rejection or Abandonment**: If you experienced neglect or emotional abandonment as a child, situations where you feel ignored, dismissed, or rejected can trigger intense feelings of inadequacy, loneliness, or anger.
- **Criticism or Judgment**: If you were frequently criticized or felt that your actions were never good enough, you may feel defensive or hurt when others criticize you, even if the feedback is constructive.
- **Feelings of Insecurity or Incompetence**: Growing up in an environment that emphasized perfectionism or unrealistic standards can make you overly sensitive to any perceived failure or mistakes, causing feelings of inadequacy or shame when you don't meet expectations.
- **Lack of Control**: If you were raised in an environment where you had little control over your life or decisions, situations where you feel powerless or out of control can trigger feelings of anxiety, helplessness, or frustration.
- **Conflict or Confrontation**: If you grew up in an environment where conflict was intense or unresolved, you may

react strongly to even mild disagreements, feeling threatened or unsafe.

- **Loss or Abandonment**: Early experiences of loss, whether through physical separation, death, or emotional neglect, can cause a trigger response when you feel that loss is being repeated or mirrored in current situations.

How Emotional Triggers Connect to Your Inner Child

Emotional triggers are often linked to unresolved issues from childhood. The reactions you experience may not always reflect the current situation but rather the emotional wounds that were never fully healed from your early years. The intensity of the response is often a sign that the emotional wound from your childhood is being reactivated.

For example:

- If you were ignored or dismissed as a child, an adult ignoring or dismissing you may evoke feelings of deep rejection or worthlessness, triggering an intense emotional response.
- If you were never allowed to express your emotions as a child, you may feel overwhelmed or explode in response to small emotional frustrations, as your inner child is trying to express itself.

These emotional reactions can be distressing and confusing, especially when they seem disproportionate to the current event. However, they are simply signals from your inner child that healing is needed in that particular area.

Identifying Your Own Emotional Triggers

The process of identifying your emotional triggers involves paying close attention to the emotional responses you experience in various situations. Here are some ways to identify your triggers:

- **Pay Attention to Intense Emotional Reactions**: When you experience a strong emotional reaction, especially if it feels out of proportion to the situation, take note of it. Ask yourself, *What about this situation feels familiar?* or *When have I felt this way before?*
- **Examine Past Experiences**: Look for patterns in your emotional reactions. Do certain situations repeatedly trigger similar emotions? What were your childhood experiences like in those areas? For example, if you feel abandoned when someone cancels plans, it may be linked to childhood experiences of emotional neglect.
- **Track Physical Sensations**: Sometimes, your body will give you clues before your mind registers the emotional trigger. You might feel your heart race, your stomach churn, or your body

tense up in response to certain situations. These physical cues can signal that an emotional trigger is being activated.

- **Consider the Underlying Fear or Need**: Emotional triggers are often connected to unmet childhood needs or fears. Is there a need for validation, love, safety, or control that is being triggered in the current situation? Understanding the underlying need can help you trace the trigger back to its source.

Working Through Emotional Triggers

Once you identify your emotional triggers, the next step is to work through them. Healing from these triggers involves not only understanding their origins but also learning how to respond to them in a healthier, more grounded way. Here are some steps to help:

- **Acknowledge the Trigger**: When you recognize that you're being triggered, take a moment to pause and breathe. Acknowledge that the emotional response you're experiencing is coming from an old wound and that it may not be reflective of the present moment.
- **Reframe Your Thoughts**: Challenge the old beliefs or narratives that are being triggered. For example, if you're triggered by criticism, remind yourself that you're worthy of respect, and that constructive feedback is not an attack on your worth.

- **Use Grounding Techniques**: Grounding exercises can help you stay connected to the present moment and prevent you from being overwhelmed by your emotions. Try deep breathing, mindfulness, or focusing on your senses to regain control.
- **Validate Your Inner Child**: Offer compassion to your inner child when you're triggered. Reassure them that they are safe now, and that the situation is not the same as it was when the original wound occurred. This kind of self-validation is key in the healing process.
- **Seek Professional Support**: Working with a therapist or coach can be especially helpful when dealing with intense emotional triggers. Techniques such as cognitive-behavioral therapy (CBT) or trauma-focused therapy can help you uncover the origins of your triggers and teach you how to respond in healthier ways.

Part 3:

Reparenting Your Inner Child

9: What Is Reparenting?

Reparenting is a therapeutic process that involves nurturing, healing, and taking care of your inner child—the part of you that holds onto the emotional experiences, needs, and memories from your childhood. It's a form of self-care where you assume the role of a loving and compassionate parent to your inner child, providing the care, support, and validation that may have been missing during your formative years.

The concept of reparenting is rooted in the idea that many of us carry unresolved emotional wounds from childhood that continue to impact our adult lives. These wounds may have resulted from neglect, emotional abandonment, criticism, or unmet needs. Reparenting aims to heal these wounds by re-creating a nurturing and safe environment within yourself, giving your inner child the love, attention, and validation it needs to thrive.

The Need for Reparenting

As children, we often rely on our caregivers—parents, teachers, and other adults—to provide us with love, protection, and guidance. However, when these needs are unmet, or when we experience neglect or abuse, the emotional needs of our inner child can be left unaddressed. These unmet needs create wounds that persist into adulthood, often manifesting as emotional struggles, self-doubt, anxiety, or unhealthy patterns of behavior.

Reparenting is essential because it allows us to heal from the past by giving our inner child the care and attention it was denied. By consciously parenting ourselves with love, patience, and understanding, we can rebuild the emotional foundation that supports our growth, well-being, and healthy relationships.

The Role of the Inner Child

The inner child refers to the part of us that holds onto childhood memories, experiences, and emotions. It is the childlike, vulnerable part of our psyche that carries the emotional impressions formed during our early years. While the inner child is often associated with innocence and joy, it can also hold onto pain, fear, and sadness.

The inner child is an integral part of our emotional well-being, and how we treat it can affect how we navigate the world as adults. When we neglect or suppress our inner child, we may struggle with unresolved emotions, trauma, or patterns of behavior that limit our potential.

Through reparenting, we can reconnect with and nurture this inner child, allowing it to heal and thrive. In doing so, we can improve our emotional health, self-esteem, and overall sense of happiness.

The Process of Reparenting

Reparenting involves intentionally stepping into the role of a compassionate parent to your inner child. This process requires a conscious effort to understand the emotional needs of your inner child and provide it with the support and care it needs. Below are some key steps involved in the reparenting process:

- **Acknowledge the Inner Child**: The first step is to recognize that your inner child exists and that it carries unresolved emotions and wounds. By acknowledging its presence, you open the door to healing.
- **Identify Unmet Needs**: Reflect on the emotional needs that were unmet during your childhood. What did you long for as a child? Did you need more love, attention, validation, or protection? Identifying these unmet needs is crucial in the reparenting process.
- **Offer Compassionate Parenting**: Now that you've identified the needs of your inner child, the next step is to parent yourself with compassion. Speak to your inner child with love and understanding, offering comfort and reassurance. This can involve both words and actions, such as writing affirmations or creating a safe space within yourself where your inner child can feel heard and loved.
- **Provide Nurturing Care**: Just like a loving parent, reparenting involves offering the care and protection your inner child requires. This may mean setting healthy boundaries, practicing self-care, and ensuring that your emotional needs are met in a nurturing way.

- **Heal Past Wounds**: As you engage in reparenting, it's important to revisit and heal past emotional wounds. This may involve forgiving yourself, letting go of shame, and reprocessing difficult memories. Through reparenting, you can provide the healing and validation your inner child may not have received in the past.

How Reparenting Benefits Your Healing Journey

Reparenting is a powerful tool for healing and growth, offering numerous benefits:

- **Emotional Healing**: By addressing the emotional wounds from childhood, reparenting allows you to heal deep-seated pain, anger, or sadness that may have been holding you back.
- **Increased Self-Worth**: When you nurture your inner child and meet its needs, you begin to recognize your inherent worth. This process fosters greater self-love and self-compassion, which improves self-esteem and confidence.
- **Breaking Unhealthy Patterns**: Reparenting helps you break free from unhealthy behavior patterns that may have been learned in childhood, such as people-pleasing, perfectionism, or self-sabotage.
- **Improved Relationships**: As you heal your inner child, you may notice improvements in your relationships. When you're

able to offer yourself love and care, you're better able to give and receive love in your relationships with others.

- **A Sense of Safety and Stability**: Reparenting allows you to create a safe and stable emotional environment within yourself, fostering a sense of security and peace. This inner stability helps you face life's challenges with resilience.

Reparenting Techniques and Practices

There are several techniques and practices that can help you engage in the reparenting process:

- **Journaling**: Writing letters to your inner child or journaling about your childhood experiences can help you process emotions and offer the care and comfort your inner child needs. Try writing a letter of love, reassurance, or forgiveness to your younger self.
- **Visualization**: Visualizing yourself as a child can help you connect with your inner child. Picture yourself comforting and nurturing your younger self, offering love and validation.
- **Affirmations**: Repeating positive affirmations like "You are loved," "You are safe," and "You are enough" can help reprogram your inner dialogue and heal old wounds.
- **Therapy or Coaching**: Working with a therapist or coach who specializes in inner child work can provide guidance and support as you reparent yourself.

- **Mindfulness and Meditation**: Practicing mindfulness or meditation can help you stay present with your emotions and create a nurturing environment for your inner child to heal.

10: Developing Self-Compassion

Self-compassion is the practice of treating yourself with the same kindness, understanding, and care that you would offer to a loved one in times of struggle or pain. It involves recognizing your own suffering, offering yourself support, and refraining from

self-criticism. In the context of inner child recovery, developing self-compassion is crucial for healing past wounds, as it helps you replace negative self-talk with positive, nurturing thoughts. Many of us are conditioned to be overly critical of ourselves, especially if we experienced neglect or harsh treatment during childhood. Self-compassion is a powerful tool to break these harmful patterns and embrace self-kindness.

What is Self-Compassion?

Self-compassion involves three key components:

- **Self-Kindness**: Treating yourself with warmth, gentleness, and understanding, especially when you're facing difficulties or setbacks. Instead of harshly judging yourself, self-kindness encourages you to respond to your struggles with empathy and care.
- **Common Humanity**: Recognizing that suffering, mistakes, and imperfection are part of the human experience. Instead of

isolating yourself in moments of pain, self-compassion reminds you that you are not alone in your struggles; all people face difficulties and challenges.

- **Mindfulness**: Being present with your feelings without over-identifying with them or pushing them away. Mindfulness allows you to observe your emotional state with a balanced perspective, acknowledging both the pain and the potential for healing.

In short, self-compassion is about treating yourself with the same care and respect that you would show to a loved one who is hurting. It's an essential practice for healing your inner child and rebuilding your emotional resilience.

The Importance of Self-Compassion in Inner Child Healing

For those who have experienced childhood trauma, neglect, or emotional wounds, self-compassion serves as a bridge to healing. The inner child often carries a great deal of emotional pain, shame, and self-criticism. These feelings can stem from past experiences where love, care, or validation was lacking. By developing self-compassion, you can offer your inner child the nurturing and emotional support that may have been absent during those formative years.

When you show self-compassion, you allow yourself to:

- **Release shame**: Self-compassion helps you understand that everyone makes mistakes and that being imperfect is a natural part of being human.
- **Heal emotional wounds**: The inner child's wounds can be soothed through kind and gentle self-talk, which allows you to rewrite the painful narrative you may have internalized during childhood.
- **Increase emotional resilience**: By responding to yourself with understanding and care, you foster the emotional strength needed to face life's challenges with greater calm and clarity.

How Self-Compassion Affects Your Inner Child

Your inner child is the part of you that holds onto the emotional experiences of your early years. When you practice self-compassion, you provide the love and emotional safety that your inner child may have missed. This process of re-parenting through self-compassion helps your inner child heal from past hurts and feel validated, heard, and supported.

By developing self-compassion, you create a nurturing inner environment where your inner child can feel safe and loved. This allows your inner child to express itself freely, process past trauma, and develop a healthier emotional foundation. Essentially, practicing self-compassion is like reparenting yourself with unconditional love and care.

How to Cultivate Self-Compassion

Here are several practical ways to cultivate self-compassion:

- **Practice Self-Kindness**: Be gentle with yourself when things go wrong. Instead of criticizing yourself, offer yourself words of comfort like "It's okay. I'm doing my best." Recognize that mistakes and setbacks are part of the human experience, not a reflection of your worth.
- **Write a Compassionate Letter to Yourself**: Take a moment to write a letter to yourself from the perspective of a loving, understanding parent. Address your struggles and offer words of encouragement, comfort, and love. This practice helps you reinforce the message that you deserve kindness and compassion.
- **Mindful Self-Reflection**: Set aside time to reflect on your emotions without judgment. When you experience negative emotions, acknowledge them and gently ask yourself what they are trying to teach you. Respond with compassion rather than judgment, such as saying, "I understand that I'm feeling upset right now, and that's okay."
- **Affirmations**: Use affirmations to remind yourself of your worth and your right to love and care for yourself. Repeating phrases like "I am enough," "I deserve love and respect," and "I

treat myself with kindness" can gradually shift your mindset and foster a deeper sense of self-compassion.

- **Release Negative Self-Talk**: Pay attention to your inner dialogue. When you catch yourself being self-critical, gently shift your thoughts toward self-kindness. For example, if you think, "I'm such a failure," replace it with, "I made a mistake, but I am still worthy of love and respect."
- **Seek Therapy or Support**: If you're struggling to practice self-compassion, working with a therapist can help. Therapy can help you identify negative patterns of thought and behavior, teach you how to respond with kindness, and provide a safe space to explore and heal your inner child's wounds.

Common Challenges in Developing Self-Compassion

Developing self-compassion can be challenging, especially for those who were not shown compassion in their childhood. It can feel foreign or uncomfortable to be kind to yourself when you're used to harsh self-criticism or feeling undeserving of love.

Here are some common challenges people face when developing self-compassion:

- **Self-Doubt**: You may feel like you're not deserving of compassion or that it's selfish to prioritize your own well-being. Remember that self-compassion is not about being self-centered; it's about treating yourself with the same love and care you would give to others.

- **Resistance to Change**: Changing ingrained patterns of thought and behavior can be difficult. Your inner critic may fight against self-compassion, but it's important to push through that resistance. Over time, self-compassion will become more natural.
- **Fear of Vulnerability**: Self-compassion requires vulnerability. You may be afraid that acknowledging your struggles or showing kindness to yourself will make you weak or expose your flaws. In reality, self-compassion fosters strength, emotional resilience, and healing.

11. Creating Safety and Boundaries for Your Inner Child

Creating safety and boundaries for your inner child is one of the most important steps in the healing process. Many of us, especially those who have experienced childhood trauma or emotional neglect, have learned to operate in environments where we didn't feel safe, valued, or protected. This lack of safety can carry over into adulthood, where we may struggle with setting healthy boundaries or feel vulnerable in relationships or situations that remind us of past wounds.

In inner child work, creating safety means providing your inner child with the protection and reassurance it may have lacked growing up. Setting boundaries involves recognizing what is emotionally, mentally, and physically healthy for you, and being assertive in protecting yourself from harmful people, behaviors, and situations.

Why Safety Is Essential for Your Inner Child

Safety is foundational for healing. Without a sense of emotional or physical safety, it's impossible for the inner child to feel supported, seen, or cared for. When your inner child feels safe, it can begin to process old wounds, release trapped emotions, and heal. Safety also allows you to rebuild trust in yourself and others, which is crucial for cultivating healthy relationships.

The concept of safety for your inner child involves:

- **Emotional Safety**: The ability to express your feelings without fear of judgment or rejection.
- **Physical Safety**: Protecting yourself from physical harm, whether that means leaving toxic environments or taking steps to ensure your well-being.
- **Psychological Safety**: The freedom to think and feel without fear of criticism or invalidation.
- **Relational Safety**: Having relationships where trust, respect, and care are mutually shared, free from manipulation, control, or abuse.

Creating emotional and psychological safety is especially important for those who have experienced neglect, abuse, or emotional unavailability from caregivers, as the inner child often carries deep scars of feeling unsafe or unworthy.

How Boundaries Protect Your Inner Child

Boundaries are like walls of protection for your inner child. They define what is acceptable and unacceptable in terms of how others treat you, as well as how you treat yourself. By setting clear boundaries, you create a space where your inner child can feel safe and secure without being overwhelmed by the emotional demands or harmful behavior of others.

Boundaries come in many forms:

- **Physical Boundaries**: These are boundaries related to your body, such as choosing who you allow into your personal space and how you protect your physical well-being.
- **Emotional Boundaries**: Emotional boundaries involve recognizing your own emotions and protecting yourself from others' emotional energy, manipulation, or abuse. This includes not allowing others to dictate how you should feel.
- **Mental Boundaries**: These boundaries protect your thoughts and beliefs. They involve standing firm in your values and not allowing others to pressure or invalidate your thinking.
- **Time Boundaries**: Setting limits on how much time you spend on others' needs and prioritizing your own well-being.
- **Energy Boundaries**: These involve protecting your emotional energy by not overextending yourself or engaging with energy-draining people or situations.

By setting boundaries, you help your inner child feel safe and protected from external threats, as well as any inner conflicts or self-destructive behaviors that might have developed as a result of past trauma.

Practical Steps for Creating Safety for Your Inner Child

Creating safety for your inner child requires both inner and outer work. Here are some practical steps to nurture your inner child's sense of safety:

- **Visualize a Safe Place**: One powerful tool for creating safety is visualization. Close your eyes and imagine a place where you feel completely safe and secure. This could be a peaceful forest, a cozy room, or a calming beach. Picture your inner child in this place, free from harm, surrounded by love and warmth. Visit this mental safe space whenever you need to feel grounded or protected.
- **Practice Grounding Techniques**: Grounding techniques help you reconnect with the present moment and protect yourself from overwhelm. When you feel unsafe or triggered, try practices like deep breathing, mindfulness, or physical grounding (e.g., placing your feet firmly on the floor). This helps your inner child feel less anxious and more in control of the environment.
- **Affirm Your Worth and Safety**: Use affirmations to reinforce the safety and security you deserve. Repeat statements like "I am safe," "I protect myself with love," or "My needs matter" to remind yourself and your inner child that safety is your right.
- **Create Safe Relationships**: Surround yourself with people who respect your boundaries and offer emotional safety. Engage in relationships where trust and care are reciprocated, and avoid

those who are emotionally abusive or toxic. Having these safe spaces helps your inner child feel supported in real life.

- **Nurture Your Physical Safety**: Take steps to ensure your physical safety, especially if you are in a toxic or abusive environment. This could mean leaving an unhealthy relationship, finding a safe space to live, or reaching out for professional help if necessary.
- **Self-Soothing Practices**: Develop self-soothing practices to calm your inner child during moments of distress. This could involve comforting rituals like taking a warm bath, listening to calming music, or engaging in an activity that brings you joy and peace.

How to Set Healthy Boundaries for Your Inner Child

Setting boundaries involves recognizing your emotional limits and protecting your inner child from further harm. Healthy boundaries give you the strength to say "no" when needed, stand up for yourself, and prevent others from violating your emotional, mental, and physical space. Here are some tips for setting and maintaining healthy boundaries:

- **Identify Your Needs**: Before you can set boundaries, you must know what your needs are. Take time to reflect on your emotional, physical, and mental needs. What makes you feel safe? What drains your energy? What do you need to feel loved and respected? Identifying these needs is the first step in setting healthy boundaries.

- **Communicate Clearly and Assertively**: Once you've identified your needs, it's important to communicate them clearly to others. Assertive communication means expressing yourself confidently and respectfully without being passive or aggressive. For example, saying "I need some quiet time" or "I'm not comfortable with that behavior" allows you to set boundaries without guilt.
- **Be Consistent**: Setting boundaries is a process, and consistency is key. If someone crosses your boundaries, gently but firmly remind them of your limits. Consistency helps reinforce the message that your emotional safety matters and deserves respect.
- **Honor Your Boundaries**: The most important step in maintaining boundaries is honoring them yourself. Don't over-extend yourself or compromise your needs to please others. Your inner child deserves to feel safe and valued, and that starts with you honoring your own limits.
- **Practice Self-Compassion**: Setting boundaries may feel uncomfortable or challenging at first, especially if you're used to people-pleasing or neglecting your own needs. Be kind to yourself during this process, and remember that boundary-setting is an act of self-love and care.

12. Practicing Positive Self-Talk

Positive self-talk is an essential practice for healing your inner child and reshaping your emotional and mental landscape. The way you speak to yourself has a powerful impact on your self-esteem, mental well-being, and overall healing journey. For many people, especially those who've experienced childhood trauma or emotional neglect, negative self-talk can be a habitual response that reinforces feelings of shame, guilt, and unworthiness. Practicing positive self-talk helps break this cycle by replacing harmful, self-critical thoughts with kinder, more affirming messages.

When you engage in positive self-talk, you are nurturing your inner child with words of love, encouragement, and validation. This practice not only supports emotional healing but also empowers you to embrace your worth and potential.

Understanding the Power of Self-Talk

Self-talk refers to the internal dialogue you have with yourself, whether it's conscious or unconscious. This inner conversation can be a reflection of your past experiences, beliefs, and how you perceive yourself. When you have negative self-talk, you may hear phrases like:

- "I'm not good enough."
- "I'll never succeed."

- “I don’t deserve love.”
- “I’m a failure.”

These thoughts, often rooted in childhood wounds or trauma, can significantly impact your emotional health and prevent healing. On the other hand, positive self-talk can transform your mindset, boost your confidence, and help you build a compassionate relationship with yourself.

Positive self-talk involves replacing negative or self-limiting thoughts with affirmations, supportive messages, and kinder perspectives. This shift in thinking helps you feel more empowered, capable, and worthy of love and respect.

Why Positive Self-Talk Is Crucial for Inner Child Healing

Your inner child carries the emotional experiences of your past, including any messages you received about your worth, identity, and potential. If you grew up in an environment where you were criticized, invalidated, or neglected, your inner child may have internalized negative beliefs about who you are and what you deserve.

Positive self-talk is essential for healing your inner child because it:

- **Reduces Self-Criticism**: Negative self-talk often stems from past emotional wounds, such as harsh criticism from caregivers.

Positive self-talk can counteract this by offering kindness and understanding.

- **Boosts Self-Worth**: When you speak to yourself with compassion, it reinforces your inherent value and reminds you that you are deserving of love and respect, just as you are.
- **Promotes Emotional Resilience**: Positive self-talk helps you stay emotionally strong, especially when faced with challenges. It encourages you to view setbacks as opportunities for growth, not as evidence of your inadequacy.
- **Encourages Healing**: Healing your inner child involves reprogramming old, limiting beliefs. By practicing positive self-talk, you replace the negative narratives of the past with affirmations of love, acceptance, and encouragement.

How to Practice Positive Self-Talk

Practicing positive self-talk is a gradual process that requires mindfulness and intention. Here are some effective ways to cultivate this practice in your daily life:

- **Become Aware of Your Self-Talk**: The first step in changing your inner dialogue is to become aware of what you're saying to yourself. Pay attention to moments when you feel self-critical or discouraged. Notice the specific phrases or thoughts that arise. This awareness will help you catch negative self-talk and replace it with positive alternatives.

- **Challenge Negative Thoughts**: When you notice negative thoughts, challenge their validity. Ask yourself:
  - Is this thought based on facts or assumptions?
  - Would I say this to a friend or loved one?
  - How can I reframe this thought in a more positive light?

For example, if you think, "I always mess things up," challenge it by reminding yourself, "I've made mistakes, but I'm learning and growing."

- **Use Affirmations**: Affirmations are positive statements that reinforce your worth and potential. Repeating affirmations daily can rewire your brain to focus on the positive aspects of yourself and your life. Some examples of affirmations include:
  - "I am worthy of love and respect."
  - "I am capable of achieving my goals."
  - "I am enough, just as I am."
  - "I trust myself to make decisions that support my well-being."
- **Practice Self-Compassionate Language**: Instead of being harsh with yourself when you make a mistake, practice using self-compassionate language. For example, if you fail at something, instead of saying, "I'm a failure," try saying, "I made a mistake, but I can learn from it and do better next time."

- **Use "I Am" Statements**: "I am" statements are a powerful way to affirm your positive qualities. For example:
    - "I am resilient."
    - "I am deserving of happiness."
    - "I am learning and growing every day."

These statements help you cultivate a sense of self-worth and remind you of your strengths.

- **Surround Yourself with Positive Influences**: The people and environments you interact with can influence your self-talk. Surround yourself with individuals who uplift you and support your growth. Engage in activities or read books that promote positivity, self-love, and healing.
- **Practice Gratitude**: Shifting your focus from what you lack to what you appreciate can improve your overall mindset. Practice gratitude by acknowledging the things in your life that bring you joy, fulfillment, or peace. For example:
    - "I'm grateful for my health."
    - "I'm thankful for the people who love and support me."
    - "I appreciate my ability to overcome challenges."
- **Visualize Success**: Take a few moments each day to visualize yourself succeeding in your goals. Picture yourself feeling confident, happy, and proud of your accomplishments. Positive

visualization can reinforce positive self-talk and motivate you to take action toward your dreams.

Common Challenges in Practicing Positive Self-Talk

While positive self-talk is a powerful tool, it can be challenging to practice consistently, especially if negative self-talk has been a habit for many years. Some common challenges include:

- **Deeply Ingrained Negative Beliefs**: If you've carried negative beliefs about yourself for a long time, it can feel difficult to believe positive statements about yourself. Start small by identifying one area where you can begin to challenge a negative belief.
- **Resistance to Change**: Changing your inner dialogue takes time and effort. You may encounter resistance from your inner critic, who may tell you that you're "fooling yourself" or "not being realistic." Keep practicing and be patient with yourself. Over time, positive self-talk will become more natural.
- **Perfectionism**: If you have perfectionistic tendencies, you might find it hard to accept yourself as you are. Remember, positive self-talk is not about being perfect—it's about being kind to yourself through the ups and downs of life.

Part 4:

Healing Through Connection

13: Rewriting Your Inner Child's Story

Rewriting your inner child's story is a powerful step in the healing process, as it involves changing the narrative you've carried about yourself for years. For many people, the story they tell themselves about their childhood may be filled with pain, neglect, abandonment, or other forms of emotional trauma. This narrative can shape how you perceive yourself in adulthood, affecting your self-worth, relationships, and ability to trust others. Rewriting your inner child's story is about reclaiming your power, reframing past experiences, and choosing to see yourself as a survivor, not a victim.

This process allows you to heal the wounds that your inner child carries by replacing limiting beliefs and negative narratives with empowering, positive stories. It is not about forgetting the past, but about rewriting it with new perspectives that honor your growth, resilience, and strength.

Why Rewriting Your Inner Child's Story Is Important

The stories we tell ourselves about our past shape how we move forward in life. For many, childhood experiences of neglect, abuse, or emotional pain have been internalized into an ongoing narrative of not being good enough, lovable, or capable of achieving success. This story can become a self-fulfilling prophecy, affecting everything from personal relationships to career choices and emotional health.

Rewriting this story is important because it:

- **Empowers You to Take Control**: When you rewrite your inner child's story, you take control of the narrative, choosing to no longer be defined by past trauma or limitations. You are the author of your life, and you get to decide how the story ends.
- **Heals Emotional Wounds**: Rewriting the narrative helps heal the emotional wounds carried from childhood. By reframing past experiences, you release old patterns and beliefs that no longer serve you.
- **Reduces Shame and Guilt**: Many people with a wounded inner child carry shame or guilt about their past. Rewriting the story allows you to release feelings of unworthiness and self-blame, helping you cultivate self-compassion and acceptance.
- **Fosters Resilience**: As you rewrite your inner child's story, you acknowledge the strength and resilience that allowed you to survive difficult experiences. You recognize that, despite the challenges, you have the capacity to heal and thrive.

How to Begin Rewriting Your Inner Child's Story

Rewriting your inner child's story involves both emotional reflection and creative visualization. Here's how to begin the process:

- **Acknowledge the Old Story**: The first step in rewriting your inner child's story is to recognize and acknowledge the old narrative. What have you been telling yourself about your childhood, your worth, or your capabilities? Write down the key themes and messages of the old story. For example:
    - "I was never good enough for my parents."
    - "I wasn't loved the way I needed."
    - "I always had to take care of myself because no one else did."

By acknowledging these beliefs, you bring them into the light where you can begin to transform them.

- **Reframe the Narrative**: Once you've identified the old story, begin to reframe it. This doesn't mean minimizing your pain or pretending that everything was okay—it means seeing the story from a different perspective. Reframe the negative beliefs and messages into empowering ones. For example:
    - "I did my best with the love and resources I had."
    - "Even though I wasn't nurtured in the way I needed, I have learned how to nurture myself."
    - "I have survived difficult experiences, and I am stronger because of them."

Reframing is about recognizing your strength, resilience, and growth rather than focusing solely on the pain or limitations.

- **Create a New Story**: Now, it's time to write a new story. Imagine your life as a book, and you have the power to rewrite the chapters. What would the new story look like? In this new story, your inner child is loved, supported, and protected. The challenges you faced become part of the journey that led you to develop wisdom, compassion, and resilience. Some examples of new storylines might be:
    - "Despite the challenges I faced, I always found ways to keep going."
    - "My past does not define me; I am creating a new, empowering story."
    - "I am deserving of love and care, and I give that love to myself now."

In your new story, you are the hero of your own life—someone who faced adversity and emerged stronger, wiser, and more compassionate.

- **Visualize Your New Story**: Visualization is a powerful tool for rewriting your inner child's story. Close your eyes and imagine the new narrative playing out in your mind. Picture yourself as a child, surrounded by love, support, and care. See yourself overcoming challenges, finding healing, and growing into the person you are today. Visualize the love and care you give to your inner child now as an adult. This visualization helps your mind and body embody the new story, integrating it into your emotional being.

Integrating the New Story into Your Life

Rewriting your inner child's story is a transformative process, but the work doesn't stop with reframing and visualization. To fully integrate the new story into your life, you must:

- **Practice Self-Acceptance**: Embrace the new story by practicing self-acceptance. When you encounter feelings of shame, guilt, or self-doubt, remind yourself of the new narrative. Say to yourself, "I am not defined by my past; I am creating a future based on love, strength, and possibility."
- **Heal Through Action**: Take action that supports the new story. This might mean setting healthier boundaries, pursuing goals that align with your values, or surrounding yourself with people who support your growth. By living in alignment with your new story, you reinforce its power.
- **Reaffirm Your New Story Daily**: Use daily affirmations to remind yourself of your new narrative. Repeating affirmations like, "I am worthy of love," "I am healing every day," or "I am in control of my life's story" will help solidify the new beliefs you are forming.
- **Reflect on Your Progress**: Periodically reflect on how your new story is shaping your life. What changes have you noticed

in your thoughts, emotions, and actions? How has your relationship with your inner child evolved? Celebrate your progress, no matter how small, and acknowledge the positive impact of your new narrative.

Overcoming Resistance to the New Story

Sometimes, the old story may feel familiar and comfortable, even though it's painful or limiting. You may face resistance from your inner critic or feel insecure about embracing the new story. Some ways to overcome resistance include:

- **Be Gentle with Yourself**: Healing takes time. If you find yourself slipping back into old patterns or thoughts, be compassionate with yourself. Remind yourself that this is part of the process, and that you are making progress every day.
- **Seek Support**: If the resistance feels overwhelming, consider seeking support from a therapist, support group, or trusted friend. Talking through your story and receiving validation can help you stay grounded in your new narrative.
- **Celebrate Small Wins**: Every time you catch yourself practicing positive self-talk or choosing an empowering action, celebrate it. These small wins will help reinforce the new story you are creating.

14: The Power of Forgiveness (Without Pressure)

Forgiveness is often seen as one of the most powerful tools for emotional healing, particularly in the journey of inner child recovery. However, the concept of forgiveness can be misunderstood, often causing feelings of pressure or obligation. Many people believe they must forgive others or even themselves in order to move forward in their healing process. This notion can feel burdensome, especially when the wounds are deep and the pain is still fresh. However, true forgiveness, when done without pressure, can be incredibly freeing and transformative, allowing you to release the grip of anger, resentment, and shame that may have been holding you back.

Forgiveness, in the context of healing your inner child, is not about condoning harmful behavior or erasing the pain caused by others. It is about giving yourself the gift of emotional freedom by letting go of the weight of past hurts. It is a process of reclaiming your power and choosing peace, without feeling rushed or obligated.

What Forgiveness Is (and Isn't)

Forgiveness is often misunderstood as something that is done for the benefit of the person who has caused harm. The truth is, forgiveness is primarily for you. It is a choice to release the emotional hold that the offense has over you, without excusing or justifying the actions that hurt you. Forgiveness does not mean:

- **Forgetting**: Forgiving doesn't require you to forget the hurt. The memories may always remain, but the emotional charge they carry can diminish.
- **Condoning Harmful Behavior**: Forgiveness is not about excusing the actions of others. It's about choosing not to let their actions continue to control your emotional state.
- **Reconciliation**: Forgiveness does not mean you have to reconnect with or trust the person who harmed you. It is a personal choice to heal, regardless of whether the relationship is restored.
- **Instant or Forced**: Forgiveness doesn't happen overnight, and it doesn't follow a prescribed timeline. Forcing yourself to forgive too soon can be damaging, especially if you haven't fully processed your emotions.

True forgiveness is a personal journey, one that can be undertaken on your own terms and at your own pace.

The Emotional Benefits of Forgiveness

Forgiveness, when practiced without pressure, has profound emotional benefits that can support your inner child's healing process. These include:

- **Emotional Freedom**: Holding on to anger or resentment can keep you emotionally trapped in the past. When you forgive, you free yourself from the negative emotions that are holding you back, allowing you to move forward in your life.
- **Release from Shame and Guilt**: Many people who experienced childhood trauma or neglect may carry a sense of shame or guilt, believing they somehow caused or deserved the pain. Forgiving others (and yourself) helps release these burdens, allowing you to embrace self-compassion and healing.
- **Healing Emotional Wounds**: The act of forgiving creates emotional space for healing. By choosing to let go of the pain of past wrongs, you open yourself up to more positive emotions, such as peace, gratitude, and love. This can significantly enhance your inner child's healing journey.
- **Empowerment**: Forgiveness is empowering because it shifts your focus from being a victim to being an active participant in your healing. You regain control over your emotions and your life by making the conscious choice to forgive and let go.

The Process of Forgiveness (Without Pressure)

Forgiveness is not a one-time event; it's an ongoing process. When you approach forgiveness without pressure, you give yourself permission to take the time you need. Here's a gentle approach to the forgiveness process:

- **Acknowledge the Pain**: Before you can forgive, it's essential to allow yourself to feel the pain. Don't rush the process of healing. Recognize the hurt, the anger, the betrayal—whatever emotions are present—and give yourself space to experience them fully. This step is vital because unprocessed pain can block forgiveness.
- **Release the Need for Revenge**: Holding onto thoughts of revenge or justice can keep you stuck in a cycle of resentment. Acknowledge that you may feel this way, but remind yourself that you are no longer bound by the past. Letting go of the need for revenge is a powerful step toward emotional freedom.
- **Understand the Impact of the Wound**: Forgiveness doesn't minimize the impact of the harm that was caused. Take time to reflect on how the wound has affected you and your inner child. This understanding can deepen your empathy for yourself and your need to heal.
- **Choose to Forgive on Your Own Terms**: Forgiveness is a choice, not a requirement. You may not be ready to forgive right away, and that's okay. Give yourself permission to take the time you need. When you do choose forgiveness, make it a conscious decision, free from any external pressure or expectation.
- **Focus on Self-Forgiveness**: Often, the hardest person to forgive is yourself. If you're carrying guilt or shame for things that were beyond your control, it's important to show

compassion to yourself. Remember that healing is a journey, and mistakes are part of being human. Be kind to yourself as you would be to a child, offering understanding, love, and patience.

- **Let Go of Expectations**: When you forgive, try to let go of any expectations of how the other person should respond. Your forgiveness is about your healing, not theirs. Whether or not the other person acknowledges your pain is irrelevant to your healing process.

How to Practice Forgiveness Daily

While forgiveness is a deeply personal process, there are daily practices you can use to support your healing:

- **Daily Affirmations of Forgiveness**: Use affirmations to remind yourself that forgiveness is a path to peace. Some affirmations might include:
    - "I forgive myself for the mistakes I've made."
    - "I release the anger I have held onto for too long."
    - "I choose to heal by letting go of the past."
    - "I am worthy of peace and emotional freedom."
- **Meditation for Forgiveness**: Meditation can help you create a space of emotional healing. Try a guided meditation focused on forgiveness, where you imagine letting go of pain and offering yourself love and compassion.

- **Writing Letters (Without Sending Them)**: Write a letter to the person who has hurt you (whether it's someone else or yourself). Express all the pain, anger, and frustration you've been carrying. When you're ready, you can choose to keep the letter for yourself, burn it, or even send it if you feel it would be healing. This practice helps release pent-up emotions and creates emotional closure.
- **Self-Care and Compassion**: Treat yourself with the love and kindness you are learning to extend to others. Practice self-care routines that nurture your inner child, such as taking time for rest, engaging in hobbies you love, and surrounding yourself with supportive people.

Why Forgiveness Should Never Be Forced

It's important to remember that forgiveness is not a requirement or a step to rush through in the healing process. Forgiving someone—or yourself—should never feel like a "should" or an obligation. If you feel pressure to forgive too soon or under duress, the process may feel inauthentic and can lead to more emotional distress. Forgiveness, when it comes naturally, should feel empowering, liberating, and healing.

Allow yourself to move through the forgiveness process at your own pace. Your healing is unique to you, and only you can decide when you're ready to forgive. Trust that, over time, as you heal, forgiveness will become a more natural and liberating part of your journey.

15: Rebuilding Trust with Yourself

Rebuilding trust with yourself is a crucial step in the process of inner child healing. Many individuals who have experienced trauma, neglect, or emotional pain during their childhood often struggle with self-doubt and lack of trust in their own judgment and abilities. This distrust can stem from the ways you were treated as a child, whether through neglect, emotional abuse, or being betrayed by those who were supposed to care for you. Rebuilding trust with yourself is about learning to believe in your own worth, decisions, and capacity for healing, regardless of past experiences. It's a process of self-empowerment that helps you reconnect with your inner child and nurture a loving, safe relationship with yourself.

Rebuilding self-trust doesn't happen overnight—it's a gradual process that requires patience, consistency, and self-compassion. The good news is that every small step you take toward trusting yourself again is a victory, and with time, you'll find yourself feeling more confident, capable, and secure in who you are.

Why Rebuilding Self-Trust Is Important

Self-trust is the foundation of healthy decision-making, emotional well-being, and personal growth. Without it, you may second-guess yourself constantly, hesitate to pursue your goals, or feel unsure of your abilities. Rebuilding trust with yourself is essential because it:

- **Empowers You to Make Decisions**: Trusting yourself means trusting your own judgment and abilities. This empowerment allows you to make decisions that are in alignment with your needs, desires, and values, without constantly seeking approval or validation from others.
- **Fosters Self-Compassion**: When you trust yourself, you treat yourself with kindness, understanding, and patience. You acknowledge your mistakes without self-criticism and offer yourself the compassion you deserve as you navigate life's challenges.
- **Promotes Healing**: Trust is integral to the healing process. When you don't trust yourself, you may feel stuck or uncertain in your recovery journey. Rebuilding self-trust helps you move forward with confidence, knowing you have the strength and wisdom to heal and grow.
- **Strengthens Your Boundaries**: Trusting yourself means you are more likely to honor your own needs, desires, and boundaries. When you trust that you deserve respect and care, you are better able to set healthy boundaries with others, which is essential for emotional well-being.

The Challenges of Trusting Yourself

Rebuilding trust with yourself can be challenging, especially if your inner child was wounded by betrayal, neglect, or mistreatment. Some common challenges people face when rebuilding self-trust include:

- **Negative Self-Talk**: If you've grown up with critical voices (either from others or within your own mind), it can be difficult to trust your decisions. You might have learned to doubt yourself or question your instincts.
- **Fear of Making Mistakes**: Many people struggle with perfectionism, fearing that any mistake means failure. This fear can lead to a lack of trust in yourself, as you become overly cautious or avoid making decisions altogether.
- **Past Traumas and Betrayals**: If your trust was broken by others, especially during childhood, it can be hard to trust yourself. You may feel that your judgment or ability to protect yourself was flawed, which leads to hesitancy when making future decisions.
- **Feeling Unworthy**: For those who suffered from neglect or emotional abuse, there can be a deep-seated belief that you're not deserving of love, respect, or care. This belief can undermine your ability to trust yourself and take actions that support your well-being.

Steps to Rebuild Trust with Yourself

Rebuilding trust is a slow, incremental process. Here are some steps you can take to begin rebuilding trust with yourself:

- **Acknowledge Past Hurt and Mistakes**: To rebuild trust with yourself, it's essential to acknowledge the pain, mistakes, and disappointments that have affected your self-esteem and self-trust. This means being honest with yourself about where you've been and how the past has impacted your view of yourself. Acknowledge the hurt that may have led to a lack of trust and allow yourself the space to process those emotions.
- **Be Patient with Yourself**: Trust isn't something that can be rushed. Allow yourself the time and patience to rebuild trust step by step. Every small success, whether it's making a decision or sticking to a boundary, is an accomplishment. Celebrate these wins, no matter how small, as they're proof of your growing trust in yourself.
- **Commit to Self-Compassion**: Self-compassion is an essential component of rebuilding trust. When you make a mistake or feel uncertain, offer yourself kindness instead of judgment. Remind yourself that you're human and that mistakes are part of the learning process. Practice treating yourself the way you would treat a friend who's going through a difficult time—with empathy, care, and encouragement.

- **Honor Your Boundaries**: One of the ways to rebuild trust with yourself is to learn to honor your boundaries. Start small by setting limits on your time, energy, and emotional resources. When you honor your own boundaries, you show yourself that you are worthy of respect and care. This builds trust by demonstrating that you can rely on yourself to protect your needs.
- **Practice Consistency**: Trust is built through consistent actions. To rebuild trust with yourself, it's important to follow through on commitments, whether big or small. Start by setting realistic goals and sticking to them, even if they are simple (e.g., setting aside time for self-care or making a decision without second-guessing).
- **Challenge Negative Self-Talk**: Pay attention to the inner critic that might be undermining your trust in yourself. When negative thoughts arise, counter them with positive affirmations. For example, if you think, "I always mess up," challenge that thought by saying, "I am capable of making good decisions, and I learn from my experiences." Gradually, you'll rewire your thoughts to support a trusting relationship with yourself.
- **Take Small, Empowering Actions**: Rebuilding self-trust starts with taking small, empowering actions. These could be as simple as making a decision on your own, following through on a commitment, or practicing self-care. Each small step builds

evidence that you can trust yourself, which strengthens your confidence and self-worth over time.

Self-Trust as a Continuous Journey

Rebuilding trust with yourself is not a destination, but a continuous journey. There will be moments when you feel uncertain or doubtful, and that's okay. What matters is that you don't abandon yourself in those moments. Keep practicing patience, compassion, and consistency. Recognize that you are worthy of trust, and that your healing is a gradual process.

As you continue to rebuild trust with yourself, you will notice an increased sense of confidence, self-reliance, and emotional strength. You'll feel more connected to your inner child and better equipped to make decisions that serve your highest good. Ultimately, rebuilding trust with yourself is about recognizing your own worth, honoring your needs, and believing in your ability to heal and grow.

16: Establishing a Loving Dialogue with Your Inner Child

Establishing a loving dialogue with your inner child is one of the most healing practices you can engage in during your recovery journey. Your inner child represents the part of you that holds the emotional experiences, memories, and wounds from your early years. For many individuals, especially those who have experienced trauma or neglect, this inner child may be in pain, feeling abandoned, or misunderstood. The process of establishing a loving, nurturing dialogue with this part of yourself is essential for healing and reclaiming your emotional well-being.

When you engage in a loving dialogue with your inner child, you are essentially building a supportive, compassionate relationship with the part of yourself that holds vulnerability, fear, and unmet needs. It's about reconnecting with the innocence and wonder that may have been lost over the years and offering that part of yourself the care, love, and understanding it truly deserves.

Understanding the Importance of Loving Dialogue

A loving dialogue with your inner child is important because it creates an emotional connection that fosters healing, self-compassion, and self-trust. When you offer a safe, caring space for your inner child to express its feelings and needs, you allow for emotional growth and healing to take place. Some benefits of establishing this dialogue include:

- **Healing Emotional Wounds**: Many of the emotional wounds from childhood can remain buried in your subconscious. Establishing a loving dialogue allows you to bring those wounds to the surface and address them with care and compassion.
- **Emotional Validation**: Often, inner children feel unheard or dismissed. By speaking lovingly to your inner child, you provide emotional validation and acceptance, letting it know that its feelings matter.
- **Promoting Self-Compassion**: When you converse lovingly with your inner child, you practice self-compassion. This helps you to release the harsh, critical voice of your inner critic and replace it with a voice of love and kindness.
- **Strengthening the Relationship with Yourself**: This dialogue strengthens your relationship with yourself by encouraging you to see yourself as worthy of care and love. As you listen to and nurture your inner child, you begin to honor your own needs and desires, ultimately fostering a deeper sense of self-love.

How to Establish a Loving Dialogue with Your Inner Child

Creating a loving dialogue with your inner child requires intention, patience, and a willingness to be vulnerable. Here are some steps to help you get started:

- **Create a Safe Space**: Before engaging in a conversation with your inner child, it's important to establish a sense of safety. This could mean finding a quiet, peaceful space where you can relax and focus. You may want to close your eyes, take a few deep breaths, and ground yourself in the present moment. You can even visualize yourself in a nurturing, safe environment, such as a peaceful garden or a cozy room, where you can interact with your inner child.
- **Acknowledge Your Inner Child's Presence**: Begin by acknowledging that your inner child is with you. You can imagine this part of yourself as a younger version of you, possibly at the age where you first experienced hurt or fear. Gently say something like, "I see you, I hear you, and I'm here for you."
- **Offer Unconditional Love and Acceptance**: Approach the dialogue with an open heart and mind. Speak to your inner child with love, understanding, and empathy. Reassure your inner child that it is safe to express its feelings. You might say,

"It's okay to feel upset. I'm here to listen to you, and I love you just the way you are."

- **Ask Open-Ended Questions**: Gently ask your inner child how it feels and what it needs. This could be as simple as, "How are you feeling right now?" or "What do you need from me?" Give your inner child the space to express itself without judgment. If you don't receive an answer right away, that's okay. Sometimes just offering the space is enough.
- **Listen with Compassion**: Allow your inner child to speak without interrupting. Be patient and let the emotions rise naturally. Remember, this is a safe space, and there's no rush. If your inner child expresses pain, sadness, or fear, validate those emotions by saying things like, "I understand that this is really hard" or "It's okay to feel this way."
- **Respond with Kindness and Nurturance**: Once your inner child has shared its feelings, respond with love and reassurance. For example, you can say, "You are safe now, and I will take care of you" or "I am proud of you for sharing that with me." Offer nurturing words that reflect your care and commitment to your inner child's healing.
- **Offer Protection and Comfort**: Sometimes, your inner child may need to feel protected and comforted. Visualize yourself as an adult offering your younger self comfort, like wrapping your arms around them or holding their hand. In these moments,

the dialogue is not just about talking—it's about providing emotional safety and reassurance.

- **Practice Regular Dialogue**: Just as any relationship needs consistent care, your relationship with your inner child requires ongoing communication. Make it a habit to check in with your inner child regularly. You can set aside time each day or week for this dialogue, or simply make it a part of your daily routine by listening to your inner child's needs throughout the day.

Overcoming Resistance to the Dialogue

It's natural to feel resistance when you first begin this practice, especially if you've been disconnected from your inner child for a long time. You might feel awkward, self-conscious, or even uncomfortable with the idea of speaking to yourself in this way. It's important to recognize that these feelings are normal and part of the healing process. Here are some tips for overcoming resistance:

- **Start Small**: If you find it difficult to engage in a full conversation, start with small moments of connection. Acknowledge your inner child briefly during meditation or journaling, or offer a simple affirmation like, "I love you."
- **Be Patient**: Healing takes time, and so does building a relationship with your inner child. Don't be discouraged if the dialogue feels difficult at first. The more you practice, the easier it will become.

- **Release Judgment**: Try to let go of any judgments you may have about how the dialogue should unfold. There is no "right" or "wrong" way to communicate with your inner child. What matters is your willingness to show up with love and care.

Building Trust Through Dialogue

The more you engage in loving dialogue with your inner child, the more trust you build between the two of you. As you consistently show up with love, patience, and empathy, your inner child will begin to feel safe and nurtured. Over time, this dialogue will transform into a deep bond based on trust, compassion, and mutual respect.

Trusting your inner child is an essential part of healing. As you listen to your inner child's voice and respond with kindness, you are reinforcing that you are reliable and capable of meeting your own emotional needs. This trust will strengthen your connection to yourself and empower you to navigate life's challenges with confidence.

Part 5:

Creative Exercises for Inner Child Healing

17: Guided Meditations for Inner Child Recovery

Guided meditations are powerful tools for healing and reconnecting with your inner child. These meditations create a space where you can explore your inner world, bring healing to your emotional wounds, and cultivate a deeper sense of compassion and safety within yourself. Through guided meditations, you can communicate with your inner child, help it feel loved and supported, and work through any trauma or emotional pain that still lingers. Meditation provides a gentle and non-threatening way to establish a loving connection with your inner child, creating a sense of emotional release, comfort, and peace.

Below are several guided meditation practices you can use to support your inner child recovery. You can choose one of these practices or combine them depending on what resonates with you most. Each meditation focuses on different aspects of inner child healing, from soothing past wounds to offering protection and nurturing love.

1. Inner Child Visualization Meditation

Purpose: This meditation is designed to help you connect with and communicate with your inner child in a safe, loving environment.

How to Do It:

- Find a comfortable, quiet place where you can relax without interruptions. Sit or lie down in a relaxed position.
- Close your eyes and take a few deep breaths. Inhale deeply through your nose, hold for a moment, and exhale slowly through your mouth. Let go of any tension with each breath.
- Imagine yourself walking into a beautiful, peaceful garden or any other place where you feel safe. This is a space that is just for you and your inner child. Notice the colors, sounds, and textures of your surroundings.
- Visualize your inner child appearing in front of you. This version of you may be a younger version, perhaps from a time when you were hurt or vulnerable. Imagine your inner child standing in front of you, either happy, sad, scared, or simply curious.
- Approach your inner child with compassion and gentleness. If your inner child seems upset or hurt, offer comfort by saying, "I'm here for you. You are safe, and I love you."
- Take a moment to ask your inner child what it needs. Listen closely, without judgment. It may want comfort, reassurance, love, or simply someone to acknowledge its pain.
- Hold your inner child's hand or embrace them if that feels right. Let them know you're here to support and protect them from now on.

- After you've shared this healing moment, gently say goodbye to your inner child, reassuring them that you will always be there when they need you. Slowly begin to come back to your body, taking a few deep breaths before opening your eyes.

2. Healing Light Meditation for Inner Child

Purpose: This meditation uses the power of light to heal emotional wounds and restore a sense of safety and peace to your inner child.

How to Do It:

- Sit or lie down in a comfortable position and close your eyes. Focus on your breathing, taking long, slow inhales and exhales to relax your body.
- Visualize a warm, healing light above your head. This light represents unconditional love and nurturing energy. Imagine this light shining down on you, slowly moving through your body.
- As the light moves down, let it pass through each area of your body, relaxing each muscle and soothing any tension. Feel the warmth and safety it provides as it travels down to your heart.

- Now, imagine that this healing light begins to move into your heart space, radiating outward to fill your entire body with warmth, safety, and love.
- Visualize this healing light flowing from your heart toward your inner child. Picture your inner child surrounded by this light, feeling its warmth and comfort.
- See the light gently healing any emotional wounds your inner child may be carrying. Feel the sense of peace and love it brings as it calms any fears or pain your inner child is experiencing.
- Spend a few moments in this space of healing and warmth, reaffirming your love and support for your inner child. Know that the light will always be there to protect and nurture you both.
- Gradually, allow the light to fade back into your heart, knowing you can call upon it whenever you need to offer healing and love to yourself.
- Take a few deep breaths and slowly return to the present moment, feeling refreshed, safe, and supported.

3. Affirmations for Inner Child Healing Meditation

Purpose: This meditation uses affirmations to nurture and rebuild the relationship with your inner child, offering unconditional love and self-compassion.

How to Do It:

- Find a quiet space where you can sit or lie down comfortably. Close your eyes and take a few deep breaths. Let go of any tension in your body.
- Begin by silently or verbally repeating the following affirmations. As you say each one, feel the words deeply and connect them with your heart.
    - "I am worthy of love and care."
    - "My inner child is safe and protected."
    - "I offer compassion and healing to my inner child."
    - "I honor my past and embrace my growth."
    - "I am here for you, my dear inner child. You are never alone."
    - "You are lovable, worthy, and enough just as you are."
    - "I trust in my ability to heal and protect you."
- Allow these words to sink in, and as you repeat them, imagine them enveloping your inner child in a warm, loving embrace.
- Visualize your inner child receiving these affirmations, their energy growing stronger and more confident with each affirmation.
- Feel a sense of love and compassion for yourself as you continue to send these affirmations to your inner child. Let the words reinforce the bond of trust, love, and safety between you and your inner child.

- After completing the affirmations, sit quietly for a few moments, letting the positive energy of the meditation settle within you. When you're ready, gently bring yourself back to the present moment.

4. Inner Child Protection Meditation

Purpose: This meditation focuses on providing protection and a sense of security for your inner child, ensuring that it feels safe and cared for.

How to Do It:

- Find a quiet, comfortable place to sit or lie down. Close your eyes and begin to focus on your breath. Allow your body to relax with each inhale and exhale.
- Visualize yourself standing in a protective circle of light. This circle is a barrier that keeps you safe from any harm, negativity, or external pressures.
- Imagine your inner child entering this protective circle. See your inner child standing beside you, feeling comforted and safe within the circle of light.
- As you stand together, visualize any fears, anxieties, or past traumas being released. Let them dissipate into the circle, where they are safely transformed by the healing light.

- Now, imagine the light expanding, forming a shield of protection around your inner child. This shield keeps them safe, offering a sense of security and peace.
- Speak gentle words of protection to your inner child, such as, "You are safe now, and nothing can harm you. You are loved and protected in this space."
- Allow your inner child to feel the full weight of this protection and reassurance, knowing that you are there to watch over and care for them.
- When you feel complete, visualize the protective circle gently fading away, knowing that the protection remains with your inner child.
- Take a few deep breaths and slowly return to the present moment, carrying the feeling of safety and security with you.

17: Visualization Practices

Visualization is a transformative tool in the healing journey, especially when it comes to reconnecting with your inner child. Through visualization, you can create a safe, nurturing space in your mind where you can meet your inner child, build trust, and foster emotional healing. By engaging in visualization practices, you not only tap into the deeper layers of your subconscious mind but also provide your inner child with the love, care, and attention it may have lacked during childhood.

Meeting your inner child through visualization allows you to nurture that younger part of yourself, offering support, understanding, and compassion. This practice helps you process past wounds, heal emotional scars, and integrate your inner child's needs and desires into your adult life.

1. Preparing for the Visualization

Before beginning any visualization, it's important to create a calm and relaxed environment. Follow these steps to prepare for a safe, healing experience:

- **Find a Quiet Space**: Choose a space where you can sit or lie down without interruptions. Make sure you're comfortable and free from distractions.
- **Set an Intention**: Decide on the intention of the visualization. For example, your goal may be to meet your inner child, heal past wounds, or offer love and reassurance.
- **Take a Few Deep Breaths**: Close your eyes, take slow deep breaths, and let go of any stress or tension. Focus on your breath, feeling each inhale fill your lungs and each exhale releasing tension from your body.

2. Visualization Practice: Meeting Your Inner Child

This visualization is designed to guide you toward meeting your inner child in a safe, loving environment. It will allow you to create an emotional connection with this younger part of yourself.

- **Close Your Eyes and Relax**: Begin by taking a few more deep breaths. As you inhale, imagine breathing in calmness, and as you exhale, release any negativity or tension.
- **Visualize a Safe, Peaceful Place**: Picture a peaceful and safe environment where you feel completely relaxed. This could be a serene garden, a cozy room, a calm beach, or a forest glade—whatever feels most comforting to you.

- **Invite Your Inner Child to Join You**: In this safe place, gently invite your inner child to join you. Picture them appearing in front of you. Your inner child might appear in the way you remember from childhood, or they might take on a different form, based on how you feel about them.
- **Observe Your Inner Child**: Take a moment to observe your inner child. What are they doing? How do they look? Are they happy, sad, or perhaps shy? Notice their emotional state without judgment. Let them be exactly as they are.
- **Approach with Compassion**: Slowly approach your inner child with love and care. Imagine your presence being gentle, safe, and non-threatening. If your inner child seems frightened or unsure, offer them comfort by speaking softly: "I'm here for you. You are safe with me."
- **Engage in a Loving Dialogue**: Ask your inner child how they're feeling, what they need, or what they wish they had received during childhood. Listen with compassion and patience, allowing your inner child to express their feelings. They may speak to you or show their emotions through images or sensations.
- **Offer Comfort and Reassurance**: Depending on what your inner child expresses, offer words of comfort. You might say, "You are loved," "I'm so proud of you," or "You don't have to be afraid anymore." Reassure your inner child that you are

there to protect, love, and nurture them from this moment forward.

- **Offer Love and Healing**: Visualize a warm, healing light surrounding both you and your inner child. This light symbolizes unconditional love and acceptance. Picture this light enveloping your inner child, soothing any hurt or fear, and filling them with warmth and safety.
- **Spend Time Together**: Allow yourself and your inner child to spend some time together. Perhaps you want to play, talk, or just sit in each other's presence. Enjoy this bond and allow your inner child to feel seen, heard, and loved.
- **Say Goodbye Gently**: When you feel ready to end the visualization, thank your inner child for their presence. Let them know that they are always welcome and that you will continue to care for them. Reassure them that you will be there for them whenever they need you.
- **Return to the Present Moment**: Slowly bring yourself back to the present moment, focusing on your breath. Take a few deep, grounding breaths to center yourself. Open your eyes when you're ready, carrying the connection with your inner child into your everyday life.

3. Additional Visualization Practices for Meeting Your Inner Child

To deepen your connection and healing with your inner child, you can try these additional visualization practices:

a. The Inner Child Embrace Meditation

In this visualization, you can imagine holding your inner child in a gentle embrace. This is a deeply nurturing practice that allows you to provide comfort and unconditional love.

- Visualize your inner child approaching you. Gently kneel down to their level and invite them into your arms.
- As you embrace your inner child, send feelings of warmth, love, and safety into them. Imagine the love you send enveloping them in light and healing energy.
- Allow your inner child to feel protected, loved, and comforted in your arms, offering them the emotional nurturing they need.

b. The Inner Child Playtime Visualization

This practice focuses on joy and play. It encourages reconnecting with your inner child through fun and carefree activities.

- Visualize yourself and your inner child engaging in a fun activity that you loved as a child. It could be playing outside, drawing, singing, or simply laughing together.

- Let the experience be light-hearted and carefree. As you engage in play, feel your inner child's joy and happiness.
- Afterward, sit with your inner child and express gratitude for the fun and laughter you shared. Let your inner child know it's always welcome to experience joy.

c. Releasing Old Emotional Wounds Visualization

This visualization is designed to help you release any lingering emotional wounds or trauma that your inner child may carry.

- Visualize a healing, compassionate light surrounding your inner child. Imagine this light gently pulling any pain or sadness from your inner child's heart.
- See the wounds, fears, or negative beliefs being gently lifted and released, transformed into pure light as they leave your inner child.
- As the light fills your inner child, feel them becoming lighter, freer, and filled with love. Send feelings of peace and healing into their heart.

19: Artistic Expression

Artistic expression is a powerful tool for healing your inner child. Through creative activities like drawing, painting, and writing, you can give voice to emotions, thoughts, and memories that may be difficult to express through words alone. These artistic practices offer an outlet for self-expression, healing, and self-discovery, allowing you to connect with your inner child in a way that feels both freeing and nurturing.

When you engage in creative activities, you create a safe space where your inner child can express themselves without fear of judgment. This process can be incredibly cathartic, as it enables you to release repressed emotions, explore past traumas, and embrace self-compassion. Additionally, creative expression allows you to tap into your imagination, reconnecting with the playful and innocent nature of your inner child.

Below are three artistic practices that can help you connect with and heal your inner child.

1. Drawing: Expressing Emotions Through Art

Drawing can be a powerful way to visually express emotions, memories, and experiences. By using simple tools like pencils, markers, or crayons, you can create images that reflect the inner workings of your heart and mind. For your inner child, drawing can serve as a safe way to process emotions that are hard to verbalize.

How to Practice:

- **Set up a Safe Space**: Find a quiet place where you can comfortably sit and draw. Gather your art supplies, whether it's paper, colored pencils, markers, or crayons.
- **Let Go of Expectations**: Begin by letting go of any expectations about what your drawing should look like. Allow your creativity to flow freely, with no judgment. This is a space for expression, not perfection.
- **Ask Your Inner Child to Guide You**: Close your eyes for a moment and ask your inner child to guide your hand. You might want to visualize a younger version of yourself holding a crayon or pencil, ready to create. Trust the process and let your inner child take the lead.
- **Draw What Feels Right**: Draw whatever comes to mind, whether it's a symbol, an image, a scene, or abstract shapes. Don't worry about making it look "good"—the purpose is to allow your inner child to express their feelings and experiences.
- **Reflect on the Artwork**: After you've finished your drawing, take a moment to reflect on what you created. What emotions

does the drawing evoke? Does it bring up any memories or insights? How does it make you feel?

- **Use Drawing for Healing**: If there are specific memories or experiences that you're working through, try drawing them out. You might create an image of a painful memory and then use colors, shapes, or symbols to transform it into something healing or empowering.

2. Painting: Using Color to Heal

Painting is another wonderful medium for emotional expression and inner child healing. The freedom of using colors and brushstrokes can help you express deep emotions in a visceral way. Painting invites you to tap into your intuition, allowing your inner child to express themselves through color and movement.

How to Practice:

- **Prepare Your Materials**: Gather your painting supplies, whether it's watercolors, acrylics, or even finger paints. Choose a canvas, paper, or any surface that feels comfortable for you.
- **Create a Safe, Relaxing Environment**: Find a space where you feel comfortable and relaxed. Play calming music, light a

candle, or add any elements that help create a peaceful atmosphere.

- **Start with a Blank Canvas**: Begin by looking at your blank canvas or paper. Don't worry about what the painting will look like at the end. Let your inner child be free to express themselves through color and form.
- **Use Colors to Express Emotions**: Choose colors that resonate with how you're feeling. For example, if you're feeling sad or vulnerable, you might choose cooler colors like blues or purples. If you're feeling joy or empowerment, you might choose brighter colors like yellow or orange.
- **Let the Brush Lead**: Use your brush (or your hands if you're working with finger paint) to allow your emotions to flow onto the canvas. Don't overthink it—let your body and hands move in rhythm with your feelings. You might create abstract shapes, symbols, or even a scene from your past that needs healing.
- **Reflect on the Process**: Once you've finished painting, take a step back and reflect on the colors and shapes you've used. What do they represent? What does your inner child need right now? How does the painting make you feel?
- **Healing Through Transformation**: If you have an image in your mind of a painful moment from childhood, you can paint it, and then gradually transform it by adding positive or healing elements. The act of transforming the image on the canvas can mirror the healing process within you.

3. Writing: Journaling and Creative Writing

Writing can be an incredibly healing practice for reconnecting with your inner child. Journaling allows you to put your thoughts and emotions into words, helping you understand and process your feelings. Creative writing, such as storytelling or poetry, can help you explore your past experiences in a way that feels liberating and expressive.

How to Practice:

- **Create a Journaling Ritual**: Find a quiet place where you can write undisturbed. Set the mood by lighting a candle, playing soft music, or having a cup of tea to relax before you begin.
- **Set an Intention**: Before you begin, set the intention for your writing. For example, you might want to write to heal a specific memory, understand a feeling, or simply express love to your inner child.
- **Write as Your Inner Child**: One approach to journaling is to write from the perspective of your inner child. Imagine that you are a child again, writing in a diary or speaking directly to an adult version of yourself. Ask questions, share fears or dreams, and express any emotions that feel present.
- **Free Writing**: Alternatively, try free writing, where you allow your thoughts and feelings to flow without editing. Write whatever comes to mind, whether it's memories from

childhood, things you've always wanted to say, or even playful stories that express your inner child's desires.

- **Write Letters to Your Inner Child**: Another healing writing exercise is to write a letter to your inner child. You can express love, reassurance, and compassion, letting your younger self know that they are worthy, safe, and loved. You might also write a letter from your inner child to your adult self, sharing their thoughts, needs, and feelings.
- **Use Creative Writing**: If you enjoy storytelling or poetry, you can create fictional stories that reflect your healing journey. Write a story where your inner child overcomes challenges, finds love, or experiences healing. This creative expression can help you reframe painful memories or create new, empowering narratives.

20: Play as a Path to Healing

Play is often seen as a simple, carefree activity, especially for children, but its importance in healing and recovery—especially for reconnecting with your inner child—cannot be overstated. Play helps to tap into the creative, spontaneous, and joyful aspects of yourself that may have been suppressed or overlooked during childhood. When we play, we create a space where we can let go of rigid thoughts, relax our boundaries, and experience freedom in our emotions and actions. Play helps you access a part of your psyche that feels unburdened by the weight of adult responsibilities, allowing the inner child to emerge and engage with the world in an authentic and healing way.

Healing through play is not about doing things perfectly; it's about reconnecting with joy, creativity, and fun—qualities that may have been lost or dimmed over the years. Play invites you to explore your emotions, express yourself without fear of judgment, and create new positive associations with your inner child.

The Therapeutic Benefits of Play

- **Emotional Release**: Play offers a safe space for expressing difficult emotions. Whether it's laughter, tears, or frustration, play allows you to release pent-up feelings that have been stored in your body and mind. For the inner child, play is a way to express those emotions in a natural, authentic way.

- **Stress Relief**: Engaging in playful activities helps lower stress and anxiety. It shifts your focus from problem-solving and worry to creativity and exploration, giving your nervous system a break and encouraging relaxation.
- **Increased Creativity**: Play taps into your creative potential. When you engage in playful activities, you allow your mind to wander, which fosters creative problem-solving and the ability to think outside the box. This creativity can then extend into other areas of your life.
- **Building Trust with Your Inner Child**: Through play, you reintroduce a sense of safety and trust into the relationship with your inner child. Play helps your inner child feel seen, heard, and accepted for who they are, which strengthens the bond between you and this younger part of yourself.
- **Reconnecting with Joy**: One of the most important aspects of play is the joy it brings. Reconnecting with the joy of play, even as an adult, helps to lift your spirits and reminds you that happiness is still possible, even in difficult circumstances.

Types of Play That Heal the Inner Child

Here are several types of play you can explore as part of your healing journey. Each one offers its own unique benefits and opportunities for reconnecting with your inner child.

- **Spontaneous Play**

  Spontaneous play involves doing something just for fun, without any agenda or plan. It could be dancing freely to music, jumping on a trampoline, or simply acting silly. The goal is to let go of control and allow your inner child to guide the experience.

  - **How to Practice**: Put on your favorite music and dance without worrying about how you look. Play a game of pretend with no structure or rules, or simply lie on the floor and make shapes with your body. Let yourself be uninhibited, allowing your body and mind to enjoy the freedom that comes with spontaneous play.

- **Creative Play**

  Creative play involves using your imagination to create or explore new possibilities. This could include drawing, painting, crafting, or building something from scratch. Creative play taps into the heart of the inner child, encouraging them to think in new ways and explore new ideas.

  - **How to Practice**: Get out your art supplies and allow yourself to draw, paint, or sculpt whatever comes to mind. The focus here is not on creating a masterpiece, but on expressing yourself freely. You can also engage in imaginative play, like pretending you're in a different world or creating a story or character.

- **Active Play**

  Active play involves physical movement and engaging the body in a way that feels joyful and freeing. This could be anything from hiking, running, playing sports, or doing yoga. For your inner child, active play allows them to feel the joy of movement and the release of energy.

  - **How to Practice**: Go for a walk in nature or take a playful exercise class. Try an activity you loved as a child, like jumping on a swing, riding a bike, or playing catch. Physical activity helps release tension, improve mood, and create a connection to the present moment.

- **Playful Storytelling**

  Storytelling is a wonderful way to tap into your inner child's imagination. This could be done through writing, telling stories aloud, or using roleplay to create a narrative. Storytelling allows your inner child to explore the world in a creative, safe space.

  - **How to Practice**: Write a story about an adventure your inner child would love to go on or create a story with no particular structure, just allowing the plot to unfold. You can also act out a scene, play a role, or make up characters in your mind. The focus is on letting your imagination run wild.

- **Nature Play**

  Nature is a powerful place to heal your inner child. Playing in nature reconnects you with the earth and its healing energy, grounding you in the present moment. Whether it's exploring the outdoors, sitting by a stream, or climbing a tree, nature offers a rich playground for healing.

- **How to Practice**: Spend time outside, reconnecting with nature. Take a walk through the woods, walk barefoot in the grass, or visit a park. Let your inner child explore the world through their senses—touch, sight, smell, and sound. You might even create a treasure hunt, go cloud-watching, or sit on a blanket and listen to the sounds around you.

The Healing Power of Play in Adulthood

As adults, we often associate play with childhood, thinking that we "should" be more serious or mature. However, engaging in play as an adult is just as important, especially for healing the inner child. When you allow yourself to play, you create space for joy, creativity, and emotional freedom—all of which contribute to healing.

The process of "letting go" and playing without judgment helps break down the walls of perfectionism and control that may have been built up over time. Play encourages you to be vulnerable, express yourself authentically, and engage in activities that nourish your soul.

Part 6:

Building a Strong Foundation for the Future

21: Nurturing Your Inner Child Daily

Nurturing your inner child is not a one-time exercise—it's a continuous process of love, care, and attention. Just like any child, your inner child needs regular affection, understanding, and validation. By nurturing this part of yourself on a daily basis, you create a loving relationship with your inner child, allowing them to feel safe, seen, and valued. This daily nurturing can promote emotional healing, increase self-compassion, and help you reconnect with your authentic self.

The process of nurturing your inner child involves treating yourself with kindness, respecting your emotions, and offering healing practices that foster self-love and self-care. It's about becoming the loving, supportive parent or guardian you needed as a child, offering reassurance and care when you need it most.

Here are some ways you can nurture your inner child each day:

1. Practicing Self-Compassion and Kindness

Self-compassion is one of the most powerful ways to nurture your inner child. When we treat ourselves with the same kindness and understanding that we would offer to a friend or loved one, we create a safe emotional environment where healing can take place.

How to Practice:

- **Speak Kindly to Yourself**: When negative self-talk arises, gently replace it with loving and compassionate words. Tell yourself that it's okay to make mistakes, to feel vulnerable, or to not have everything figured out.
- **Acknowledge Your Emotions**: Validate your emotions, whether they are positive or negative. Allow your inner child to express themselves without judgment. For example, instead of saying, "I shouldn't feel this way," try saying, "It's okay to feel sad. I am here for you."
- **Forgive Yourself**: Release any guilt or shame that may arise from past mistakes. Forgiveness is a crucial step in healing your inner child. Let go of self-blame and recognize that you are doing the best you can.

2. Daily Affirmations

Affirmations are powerful statements that can shift your mindset and foster a loving relationship with your inner child. By repeating positive affirmations daily, you reprogram your subconscious mind and reinforce self-love and compassion.

How to Practice:

- **Start Your Day with Affirmations**: Every morning, say affirmations aloud or write them down. These affirmations can be simple yet powerful, such as, "I am worthy of love," "I am enough," or "I accept and love my inner child."
- **Create Your Own Affirmations**: Write affirmations that resonate with you and your inner child's needs. For example, if you feel abandoned, an affirmation like "I am always here for myself" may be helpful.
- **Use Mirror Work**: Stand in front of a mirror and look into your own eyes as you say these affirmations. This practice helps deepen the connection with yourself and reinforces your worth.

3. Set Boundaries for Protection and Safety

Your inner child needs to feel safe in order to heal and thrive. Setting boundaries is an act of self-care and protection that helps your inner child feel secure in the present moment. Boundaries allow you to honor your feelings, needs, and desires without compromising your well-being.

How to Practice:

- **Recognize When You Need to Say No**: Whether it's in relationships, work, or personal commitments, identify when your inner child feels overwhelmed or unsafe and practice saying no. Protect your energy and emotional well-being by learning to assert your boundaries.

- **Create Emotional Boundaries**: Set emotional boundaries by recognizing when negative emotions from others are affecting you. You have the right to distance yourself from situations that are emotionally draining or toxic.
- **Protect Your Inner Peace**: Create time and space for yourself, especially in busy or stressful times. Honor your need for quiet moments, rest, and relaxation.

4. Engaging in Fun and Playful Activities

Just like any child, your inner child thrives on fun and play. Incorporating play into your daily routine brings joy and healing, allowing you to reconnect with your authentic self and experience moments of freedom. It's important to engage in activities that bring you joy, whether they are creative, physical, or simply playful.

How to Practice:

- **Find Playful Moments**: Look for opportunities to play each day, whether it's dancing in your living room, playing with a pet, or doing something creative like drawing or coloring. Allow yourself to be spontaneous and carefree.

- **Engage in Childlike Activities**: Do something that you loved as a child—whether it's jumping on a trampoline, playing a game, or watching cartoons. Reconnect with the activities that brought you joy and excitement when you were younger.
- **Incorporate Laughter**: Laughter is healing and uplifting. Watch a funny movie, listen to a comedy podcast, or spend time with people who make you laugh. Laughter is a great way to release tension and reconnect with your inner child.

5. Journaling and Reflection

Journaling is a deeply introspective activity that allows you to check in with your inner child. By reflecting on your feelings, thoughts, and experiences, you can gain insight into what your inner child needs for healing and growth.

How to Practice:

- **Write Letters to Your Inner Child**: Write a letter to your inner child, offering words of love, compassion, and reassurance. Let them know that they are safe, valued, and loved.

- **Daily Check-Ins**: Take a few minutes each day to journal about how you're feeling. Reflect on any emotional experiences that arise and offer yourself empathy and support.
- **Track Your Progress**: Keep a journal where you can track your healing journey. Reflect on moments of joy, challenges you've faced, and the steps you've taken to nurture your inner child.

6. Practice Self-Care Routines

Self-care is essential for nurturing your inner child. Taking care of your body, mind, and spirit sends a message to your inner child that they are worthy of love and attention.

How to Practice:

- **Create a Self-Care Routine**: Engage in daily self-care practices that nourish your physical, emotional, and mental health. This could include things like taking a warm bath, practicing yoga, meditating, or simply getting enough sleep.
- **Treat Yourself with Kindness**: Pamper yourself with small acts of kindness, such as enjoying a warm cup of tea, reading your favorite book, or spending time in nature.

- **Practice Mindfulness**: Mindfulness helps you stay present and aware of your inner world. Engage in mindfulness practices like meditation, breathing exercises, or mindful walking to ground yourself and calm your inner child

22: Cultivating Emotional Resilience

Emotional resilience is the ability to adapt to and bounce back from difficult or challenging emotional experiences. It's a vital quality for anyone on the journey of inner child recovery, as it helps you cope with the emotional challenges that arise during the healing process. Cultivating emotional resilience means developing a mindset and emotional toolkit that allows you to face adversity without being overwhelmed or consumed by it.

For your inner child, building resilience means learning to navigate difficult emotions in healthy ways, understanding that emotional pain doesn't define who you are, and finding the strength to heal and grow even in the face of setbacks. Resilience helps you build a sense of self-worth and confidence, which can ultimately allow you to reclaim your power and take control of your life.

By nurturing emotional resilience, you equip yourself with the tools to face life's ups and downs with grace, strength, and a sense of inner peace. Here's how to cultivate emotional resilience in a way that supports your inner child's healing journey:

1. Understanding Emotional Resilience

Emotional resilience isn't about avoiding difficult emotions—it's about learning how to manage and navigate them in a healthy and constructive way. Resilience involves acknowledging your feelings, accepting that life can be challenging at times, and using those experiences as opportunities for growth.

Key Characteristics of Emotional Resilience:

- **Self-Awareness**: Being in tune with your emotions and understanding how they influence your thoughts and actions.
- **Self-Regulation**: The ability to manage emotional reactions and responses, especially during times of stress or adversity.
- **Optimism**: Maintaining a hopeful perspective, even when things seem bleak. Resilience is about believing in your ability to overcome challenges.
- **Adaptability**: The capacity to adjust to new circumstances and find solutions, even when faced with unexpected challenges.

2. Reconnecting with Your Strengths

Your inner child may have experienced pain, loss, or rejection, which can lead to feelings of powerlessness or inadequacy. However, your inner child is also strong and resourceful. By reconnecting with the strengths and resilience you've developed throughout your life, you help restore your inner child's confidence and sense of self-worth.

How to Practice:

- **Reflect on Past Triumphs**: Take time to reflect on the times in your life when you faced challenges and overcame them. Recognize the inner strength and resilience you exhibited during those times.
- **Celebrate Small Wins**: Cultivate the habit of celebrating even the smallest victories, whether it's handling a difficult situation with grace or taking a step toward healing. Each moment of growth is a testament to your resilience.
- **Acknowledge Your Inner Strength**: Write down or speak aloud qualities about yourself that show your resilience—whether it's your ability to persevere, your adaptability, or your courage. Recognize and honor these traits as valuable sources of strength.

3. Embracing Emotional Awareness

Developing emotional resilience begins with being aware of your feelings and allowing yourself to experience them fully. When you allow yourself to feel and express your emotions, without judgment, you free yourself from the emotional suppression that can block healing. Your inner child needs to know that all feelings—whether positive or negative—are valid and deserve to be expressed in a healthy manner.

How to Practice:

- **Check-In with Your Emotions**: Regularly pause throughout your day to check in with your emotional state. Are you feeling sad, angry, anxious, or happy? Acknowledge and name your emotions without trying to change them.
- **Journaling Your Emotions**: Writing about your feelings can help release pent-up emotions and provide clarity. Try journaling about what's going on in your life and how it makes you feel, allowing your inner child to express themselves without fear of judgment.
- **Feel Without Judging**: Give yourself permission to feel without labeling or criticizing your emotions. Whether you're feeling sad, scared, or frustrated, let yourself experience those emotions fully and trust that they will pass.

4. Building Coping Skills

Developing healthy coping skills is essential for emotional resilience. These are the tools you use to manage difficult emotions in a constructive way. The more coping mechanisms you have at your disposal, the better equipped you are to deal with emotional challenges without becoming overwhelmed.

How to Practice:

- **Mindfulness and Meditation**: Mindfulness techniques help you stay grounded in the present moment, reducing anxiety and preventing overwhelming emotions. Meditation can also help you connect with your inner child in a peaceful, reflective way.
- **Breathing Exercises**: Deep breathing exercises help calm the nervous system and reduce stress. Practice diaphragmatic breathing or try box breathing to quickly regulate your emotions.
- **Seeking Support**: Don't be afraid to lean on others when you need help. Reach out to trusted friends, family, or a therapist when you're feeling emotionally stretched. Support is essential for building resilience and processing difficult emotions.
- **Healthy Distractions**: Engaging in activities that bring you peace or joy, such as walking in nature, listening to music, or practicing yoga, can help you manage overwhelming emotions and restore balance.

5. Reframing Negative Thoughts

The way you think about challenges and adversity can have a profound impact on your emotional resilience. Negative thinking patterns can contribute to feelings of helplessness and fear, while reframing those thoughts can open the door to growth, healing, and empowerment.

How to Practice:

- **Challenge Negative Thoughts**: When you catch yourself thinking negatively or catastrophizing, take a moment to challenge those thoughts. Ask yourself, "Is this thought based on fact or assumption?" "What is the worst-case scenario, and how would I handle it?"
- **Focus on the Positive**: While it's important to acknowledge difficult emotions, it's also helpful to intentionally focus on the positive aspects of a situation. Look for the lessons, the growth, or the opportunities that might arise from challenges.
- **Reframe "Failure"**: Rather than seeing setbacks as failures, view them as learning experiences. Remind yourself that failure is often a stepping stone to success, and each setback provides valuable insight into how you can grow and move forward.

6. Self-Care as Emotional Resilience

Taking care of yourself physically, emotionally, and mentally is one of the most effective ways to build emotional resilience. By practicing self-care, you replenish your emotional reserves, making it easier to cope with challenges and bounce back from difficult situations.

How to Practice:

- **Get Enough Rest**: Sleep and rest are essential for emotional regulation. Make sure you're getting enough rest each night to allow your mind and body to recharge.
- **Exercise Regularly**: Physical activity helps release endorphins, which are natural mood lifters. Regular exercise also helps reduce stress and anxiety, providing emotional relief.
- **Eat Nourishing Foods**: The food you eat plays a significant role in your emotional health. Choose nutrient-dense foods that fuel your body and mind, such as whole grains, vegetables, and fruits.

23: Creating Healthy Relationships as an Adult

Creating healthy relationships as an adult is a powerful way to nurture your inner child and foster emotional well-being. Our relationships play a critical role in shaping how we feel about ourselves, how we perceive the world, and how we interact with others. For those healing from childhood wounds, it's essential to approach relationships from a place of self-awareness, self-compassion, and a commitment to setting healthy boundaries.

Healthy relationships, whether romantic, platonic, or familial, should empower and support you rather than diminish your self-worth. They should foster open communication, trust, mutual respect, and emotional safety. As you heal your inner child, you learn to choose and maintain relationships that are aligned with your values, contribute to your growth, and nourish your emotional well-being.

Building and sustaining healthy relationships requires reflection, intention, and effort. By engaging in these practices, you create the space for deep connections that promote healing and personal growth.

1. Understanding the Importance of Healthy Relationships

Healthy relationships are foundational to emotional resilience and well-being. For someone on a healing journey, the right relationships can provide emotional support, foster self-esteem, and promote personal growth. On the other hand, toxic or unhealthy relationships can exacerbate feelings of insecurity, anxiety, and low self-worth.

Key Components of Healthy Relationships:

- **Trust**: Trust is the cornerstone of any healthy relationship. Without it, there is no emotional safety, and genuine connection is impossible. Trust is built over time through consistency, honesty, and respect.
- **Mutual Respect**: In healthy relationships, both individuals honor each other's feelings, opinions, and needs. They show empathy, listen actively, and value the other person's perspective.
- **Effective Communication**: Open, honest, and non-judgmental communication is essential. Healthy communication means expressing your needs, desires, and feelings clearly, and also listening with intention and compassion.
- **Emotional Safety**: Both parties should feel safe to express their emotions without fear of judgment or retaliation. This requires creating an environment of respect, care, and vulnerability.

2. Healing Through Boundaries

Boundaries are vital in protecting your emotional well-being and ensuring that your needs are respected in relationships. For someone healing their inner child, it's important to recognize where boundaries need to be established and practice enforcing them.

How to Practice:

- **Recognize Your Needs**: Take time to reflect on your emotional needs in relationships. What makes you feel safe, respected, and loved? What behaviors or actions feel harmful or triggering to your inner child?
- **Establish Clear Boundaries**: Be clear about your limits and communicate them assertively but with kindness. Healthy boundaries help prevent emotional exhaustion, resentment, or feelings of violation.
- **Respect Others' Boundaries**: Healthy relationships involve mutual respect for each other's boundaries. Pay attention to what your loved ones need and ensure you honor their limits as well.
- **Learn to Say No**: Saying no is a powerful way to protect your emotional energy. You don't have to say yes to everything, and it's okay to prioritize your own well-being.

3. Building Trust and Vulnerability

In healthy relationships, trust and vulnerability go hand in hand. For someone healing from inner child wounds, learning to trust others while also being vulnerable can be challenging, but it is a critical step in creating deeper connections.

How to Practice:

- **Start Small**: Building trust doesn't happen overnight. Start with small acts of openness and honesty in your relationships. Share your thoughts, feelings, and experiences gradually, allowing trust to build over time.
- **Be Honest About Your Needs**: Vulnerability requires honesty. Be clear with your loved ones about your emotional needs, and express them in a way that is respectful and non-blaming.
- **Allow Yourself to Be Seen**: Trust also means allowing others to see your authentic self—imperfections and all. Embrace your vulnerability, knowing that true connection comes from being seen for who you really are.
- **Recognize When Trust Is Broken**: If someone in your life violates your trust or repeatedly crosses your boundaries, it's important to address the issue directly. Healing involves recognizing when trust has been broken and taking steps to protect yourself.

4. Choosing Healthy Relationships

As an adult healing from childhood trauma, it's crucial to recognize the types of relationships that are healing and supportive, and those that may be harmful or toxic. Healthy relationships are built on shared values, respect, and mutual support, while toxic relationships can drain your energy, exacerbate emotional wounds, and perpetuate unhealthy patterns.

How to Practice:

- **Evaluate Your Relationships**: Reflect on the relationships in your life. Are they nurturing, respectful, and supportive? Or do they cause you stress, anxiety, or emotional pain? Trust your instincts and choose relationships that align with your needs.
- **Avoid People Who Disrespect Boundaries**: Toxic individuals may disregard your boundaries or manipulate your emotions. If you find yourself repeatedly compromising your own needs or feeling diminished in the presence of certain people, it may be time to reconsider the relationship.
- **Surround Yourself with Positive Influences**: Seek out relationships that encourage your growth and healing. Surround yourself with people who uplift you, support your dreams, and respect your journey of self-discovery.
- **Be Open to New Connections**: As you heal, you may find that your old relationships no longer serve your highest good.

Be open to forming new, healthy connections that support your healing journey.

5. Practicing Self-Love and Self-Respect in Relationships

Creating healthy relationships starts with the relationship you have with yourself. When you practice self-love and self-respect, you are better equipped to show up authentically in your relationships and attract people who will honor and value you.

How to Practice:

- **Know Your Worth**: Recognize that you are worthy of love, respect, and healthy relationships. Affirm your value regularly, and practice self-compassion when faced with challenges.
- **Don't Settle for Less**: In relationships, it's essential to never settle for treatment that is less than you deserve. Trust your worth and insist on relationships that uplift you.
- **Practice Self-Care**: Prioritize your own emotional well-being through self-care practices that nourish your body, mind, and soul. When you take care of yourself, you set an example for others about how you should be treated.
- **Set Healthy Expectations**: Understand that no relationship is perfect, and it's normal to experience challenges. However,

healthy relationships should bring more joy and growth than pain. Be realistic about your expectations and communicate openly about your needs.

6. Navigating Conflict with Compassion

Conflict is a natural part of any relationship, but how you handle it is what defines the health of the relationship. Navigating conflict with compassion and respect is essential for creating long-lasting, healthy bonds.

How to Practice:

- **Communicate Openly**: When conflict arises, address it directly rather than avoiding it. Practice open communication, and express your feelings and needs calmly and respectfully.
- **Listen to Understand**: Listen to the other person's perspective with an open mind and heart. Make an effort to understand where they are coming from before responding.
- **Stay Calm and Centered**: In heated moments, it's easy to get caught up in strong emotions. Practice staying calm, take deep breaths, and pause before reacting. This allows you to respond from a place of clarity rather than reactivity.

- **Seek Resolution, Not Victory**: The goal of resolving conflict should be finding a mutually beneficial solution, not "winning" the argument. Approach conflict with a mindset of compromise and collaboration.

24: Moving Forward

The journey of healing your inner child is not about perfection—it's about embracing your wholeness, integrating the different parts of yourself, and moving forward with a sense of empowerment, self-love, and acceptance. After spending time reconnecting with your inner child, understanding past wounds, and cultivating the emotional resilience to heal, you may now find yourself at a crossroads—feeling more connected to yourself, yet also faced with the challenge of embracing all of who you are, including the parts that may have been hurt or neglected.

Embracing wholeness means recognizing that you are not defined by your past experiences, but by your ability to move forward, heal, and grow. It involves integrating all aspects of your being—the wounded parts of your inner child, the adult you are today, and the person you are becoming—into a unified, balanced sense of self.

This process is about moving beyond shame, self-doubt, and self-judgment, and instead stepping into a space of compassion, growth, and acceptance. When you embrace wholeness, you allow yourself to fully live, experience joy, and engage with others in authentic ways. It's about living in alignment with your values, taking ownership of your healing, and cultivating an empowered mindset that supports your ongoing personal development.

Integrating the Inner Child into Your Adult Life

As you move forward in your healing journey, the key to embracing wholeness is learning to integrate your inner child into your adult life. Rather than seeing your inner child as a separate part of you, recognize that your inner child is always a part of your present self. Healing and growth are not about "leaving the past behind"—they're about learning to live fully and authentically with all aspects of your being.

How to Practice:

- **Validate Your Inner Child**: Your inner child needs to be heard, seen, and validated. As you move forward, make a commitment to regularly check in with your inner child. Acknowledge their feelings and allow them to express their emotions without judgment.
- **Embrace Playfulness and Joy**: Your inner child is the part of you that knows how to play, explore, and find joy in the simple things. As you embrace wholeness, don't forget to engage with the world in a playful and spontaneous way. Give yourself permission to experience joy without guilt.
- **Nurture Self-Compassion**: The relationship you have with your inner child is built on compassion. As you integrate this part of yourself into your adult life, continue to practice self-compassion. Treat yourself with the same love, care, and understanding that you would offer a child who's been hurt.

- **Set Healthy Boundaries for Your Inner Child**: Integration doesn't mean allowing your inner child to take over every aspect of your life. It's important to balance the needs of your inner child with the wisdom and responsibility of your adult self. Set boundaries that protect your emotional well-being while allowing space for healing.

Cultivating Ongoing Growth and Healing

Embracing wholeness is a continuous journey—healing is not a one-time event but an ongoing process. To maintain your wholeness, it's essential to nurture your personal growth, remain open to new experiences, and prioritize your emotional and spiritual well-being. This ongoing growth helps you stay connected to your true self and empowers you to live a life aligned with your values.

How to Practice:

- **Commit to Lifelong Learning**: Growth happens through learning. Whether through reading, reflection, therapy, or new experiences, make a commitment to continue learning about yourself, your emotions, and your needs.
- **Regular Self-Reflection**: Continue your practice of journaling, meditation, or other forms of self-reflection to stay

connected with your inner self. Reflect on your progress, challenges, and the ways in which you are growing.

- **Set Intentional Goals**: As you move forward, set clear and meaningful goals that align with your values and vision for your life. These goals don't have to be monumental—they can be small, everyday actions that move you closer to living in alignment with your truest self.
- **Stay Open to Change**: Embrace the idea that change is a constant. Just as you've evolved in your healing process, continue to evolve as a person. Be open to new experiences, new relationships, and new perspectives that help you grow.

Releasing Self-Judgment and Embracing Self-Acceptance

One of the most powerful aspects of embracing wholeness is letting go of self-judgment. The healing process can sometimes stir up feelings of guilt, shame, or frustration, especially if you feel like you "should be further along" or have "not done enough." These thoughts are normal but must be recognized and released in order to fully embrace your wholeness.

How to Practice:

- **Let Go of Perfectionism**: Perfectionism can hinder progress and create feelings of inadequacy. Embrace the idea that you are enough just as you are, imperfections and all. Healing is not about achieving perfection, but about growth and acceptance.
- **Practice Self-Forgiveness**: Self-forgiveness is essential in moving forward. Release any guilt or shame from your past. Understand that you were doing the best you could with the resources and knowledge available to you at the time. Offer yourself compassion and grace as you move forward.
- **Focus on Self-Acceptance**: Embrace who you are—your strengths, your vulnerabilities, your past, and your potential. Accept yourself as a whole person, worthy of love, care, and respect. This will help you show up in your relationships and life with confidence and authenticity.
- **Challenge Negative Self-Talk**: Pay attention to any negative self-talk or limiting beliefs that arise. Challenge them by reminding yourself of your inherent worth, strength, and ability to grow. Replace those negative thoughts with affirmations of self-love and compassion.

Living in Alignment with Your True Self

Embracing wholeness means living authentically, guided by your inner truth. As you move forward, make intentional choices that align with your core values and deepest desires. Trust yourself and honor the path that is uniquely yours.

How to Practice:

- **Listen to Your Intuition**: Your inner wisdom and intuition are powerful tools for guiding your life. Tune into what feels right for you, and trust that you have the ability to make decisions that support your growth and happiness.
- **Prioritize What Truly Matters**: Focus on what's truly important to you. Whether it's relationships, creativity, health, or personal growth, make sure your life aligns with the things that bring you fulfillment and joy.
- **Take Inspired Action**: Take action toward your dreams and goals, even if it feels uncomfortable at times. Embrace courage and step into the unknown, knowing that each step you take is part of your greater journey toward wholeness.
- **Live Authentically**: Live in alignment with who you truly are, not who others expect you to be. Allow your authentic self to shine through in your choices, your words, and your actions.

Conclusion

Healing your wounded inner child is not a destination—it is an ongoing journey of self-discovery, compassion, and growth. Throughout this guide, you have explored the roots of your inner child's wounds, learned how to reconnect with forgotten emotions, and discovered powerful tools to nurture and reparent yourself. You have taken courageous steps toward self-love, rewriting old narratives, and building a foundation for emotional resilience.

As you move forward, remember that healing does not happen overnight. Some days will feel lighter, while others may bring old wounds to the surface. Be patient with yourself. Your inner child does not need perfection—only your presence, understanding, and willingness to listen. The more you integrate these practices into your daily life, the stronger and more secure your connection with your inner child will become.

Healing is not about erasing the past but transforming your relationship with it. You have the power to create a life where your inner child feels safe, seen, and valued. You deserve joy, love, and emotional freedom. Keep showing up for yourself, one step at a time, and trust that every act of self-care is a step toward lasting transformation.

You are not broken—you are becoming whole. Your inner child is waiting with open arms. Embrace them, nurture them, and step into the life you were always meant to live.

www.ingramcontent.com/pod-product-compliance
Lightning Source LLC
LaVergne TN
LVHW022222200926
848481LV00006B/2071
* 9 7 9 8 3 4 8 4 9 2 4 9 6 *